AWAKE

Rise to Your Divine Assignment

By Sarah Wehrli

ENDORSEMENTS

"*Awake* is a message for the Body of Christ. God wants us to awaken out of our slumber, to our purpose and mission on this earth! People are waiting for the Church to live life fully awake. Sarah is a prophetic voice to this generation and lives the message of this book daily! She is a great inspiration to us all."

> Christine Caine, Director,
> Equip & Empower Ministries and founder,
> The A21 Campaign

"The book *Awake: Rise to Your Divine Assignment* is great and will bless multitudes. Everyone has an assignment no one else can do. Sarah has done hers well and I am so proud of her and Caleb. She has made her mother and dad especially proud."

> Dodie Osteen,
> Co-Founder of Lakewood Church

"*Awake* is a breath of fresh air to the body of Christ! I so enjoyed reading the book and seeing the heart of Sarah pour through the pages. Each chapter clearly articulates a new way you can be awakened to the things of God and live a life that is kingdom driven and meaningful to those around you. The chapter on hearing God's voice and trusting the Holy Spirit will bless you and take your intimacy with God to a new level. This book blessed me and I believe it will do the same to all who read it."

> Dr. Wendy Treat,
> Christian Faith Center,
> Seattle, Washington

"When I read Sarah's book, *Awake*, I'm taken back in time to when she was a little baby and I held her in my hands. Now I look and see what is in her hands and it is outstanding. *AWAKE: Rise to Your Divine Assignment* is for every believer. We need to get up, shake ourselves off and go forward with special anointing and use what is in our hands. What is in your hands? What is in this book for you? There are miracles in your hands. Read the book, take your time with it, underline and makes notes and let the Holy Spirit talk to you about your personal assignment. I'm very proud of Sarah and amazed at how God uses her so beautifully around the world."

> Dr. Marilyn Hickey,
> President of Marilyn
> Hickey Ministries

"When God gives us a dream, it is so that we may awaken sleeping potential and hibernating hope that is in our lives and the lives of those around us. Sarah has written a book that will encourage you to not just dream but to do. She has modeled so beautifully in her own journey a commitment to awaken to the needs of those near and far, allowing God to disturb her so she can awaken others. I am honored to call Sarah friend and I know her story will inspire you to awaken to your own."

> Charlotte Gambill,
> Abundant Life Center,
> Bradford UK

"In a world searching for meaning on dead-end streets, Sarah Wehrli awakens the desire in every human heart to soar! Her poignant stories and simple but powerful truths challenge us to let go of fear and live the life of our dreams, full of God and full of purpose!"

> Lynette Lewis,
> Speaker and Business Consultant,
> author of *Remember the Roses*

"God is truly awakening his daughters by whatever means it takes. Sarah has taken her dream and translated it into an urgent plea for all of us to rise up to our destiny. Read her words and be empowered."

Lisa Bevere, Author and Speaker,
Messenger International

"I am *so* excited about Sarah Wehrli's new book, *AWAKE: Rise to Your Divine Assignment.* In it, she conveys wisdom beyond her years and insights that are sure to stir up a deep passion within you to pursue God's purposes.

"I have watched Sarah grow up and have witnessed her awakening to God's divine assignment in each new season of life. Her strong devotion to Him and to His work is apparent to all who know her, and the words she shares are certain to inspire you!"

Tamara Graff, Co- Pastor,
Faith Family Church, Victoria, Texas

"If you have wondered why you are here on earth at this time, this book will help you see why you are here. No matter what has happened in your life, you are so valuable and needed by God.

"There are people you do not even know who will be touched by your life when you awaken to God's calling and realize that God can do anything through a yielded heart.

"Each chapter of Sarah's book will inspire and motivate you to believe and obey God."

Sharon Daugherty
Senior Pastor,
Victory Christian Center, Tulsa, OK

"Sarah and Caleb Wehrli are two of the strongest new generation leaders in America. Their lives, their family, their ministry are exemplary. Sarah's powerful book, *Awake*, is about "alignment for your assignment." She is blowing the trumpet of action, purpose, and conquest. As our nation slips further and further into oblivion, isn't it time someone said, "Wake up!" This one book could be the difference in your life being wasted or multiplied. Read it, digest it, and get it. "AWAKE, O sleeper, and rise from the dead, and Christ will shine upon you! (Ephesians 5: 14)"

> Larry Stockstill
> Pastor and Speaker
> Bethany World Prayer Center

"Sarah Wehrli is uniquely prepared to write this book. Ever since she can remember, she and her family have been soaring to heights most people never attain — not because they didn't face obstacles but because they chose to look beyond those obstacles unto Jesus and focus on what He called them to do.

Starting on page one of *Awake*, Sarah draws the reader in with her candor and authenticity, as she recounts a difficult time when God called her to rise above the pain and loss in her own life to soar even higher. She then summons us to rise up and respond to that same challenge from Jesus so that we, too, can soar to places we've not yet attained in the Lord. This book is easy to read. Every word is saturated with strength. You will be a better Christian for reading this book, especially if you take to heart its message and "awake" to what God is saying to you!"

> Rick Renner
> Teacher, Author, and Senior Pastor
> Moscow Good News Church

15 14 13 12   10 9 8 7 6 5 4 3 2 1

AWAKE: Rise to Your Divine Assignment
ISBN: 978-160683-503-6
Copyright © 2012 by Sarah Wehrli

Published by Harrison House, LLC
P.O. Box 35035
Tulsa, Oklahoma 74153
www.harrisonhouse.com

CONTENTS

ACKNOWLEDGMENTS

I want to thank my Lord and Savior Jesus Christ for awakening my heart to know Him. He is my source and the reason why I've written this book.

To my husband and best friend, Caleb, thank you for your constant love and encouragement to fulfill my assignment. I am grateful to be on this adventure with you!

To my children, Isaac and Elizabeth, you are such a joy and delight. I am excited to see your unique God-given assignment unfold!

To Andrea Graff, thank you for all you have done to help me in the editing process. You are a talented young woman and I know your future is bright!

To Carol Worley, thank you for your ideas and support in the writing process.

To Laura Straub, I appreciate your support and encouragement in the writing process of this book.

To Julie Werner, Christian Ophus, Troy and Joyce Wormell, and the whole team at Harrison House Publishers. Thank you for believing in the message of this book and for your excellent work on this project.

To my parents, Billy Joe, who is now in heaven, and my mom, Sharon Daugherty, thank you for raising me to learn how to hear

God's voice and go where He says to go. I am forever grateful for your example and for believing in the call of God on my life!

To the mentors and friends who wrote an endorsement for this book, thank you for paving the way for the next generation to move forward in the plans and purposes of God. You are heroes in the faith!

To all my friends and family, thank you for your love and support. I am honored to be running this race together with you!

1

AWAKE

In August of 2009, I had a dream that really woke me up, not just physically, but spiritually as well. In the dream, I was standing in a circle of people, and it seemed as though we were all waiting for something. It didn't take me long to realize we were waiting for orders. We had a mission to complete, and each of us was given individual assignments to fulfill. As I glanced to my right, I noticed the girl next to me was curled up in a fetal position asleep, and I thought, *Why is she sleeping? She needs to wake up! We have a job to do!*

When I got up, I sensed God was trying to speak to me. So, I asked Him what the meaning of this dream was. He said the circle of people represented the Body of Christ, and each person has a part to play and a divine assignment to fulfill (as I Corinthians 12 expounds more upon). But some have chosen to fall asleep, instead of walking in their calling because of tragedy, hurt, or fear.

He then directed me to the scripture in Isaiah 52:1-2 NIV which says, "Awake, awake, O Zion, clothe yourself with strength. Put on your garments of splendor, O Jerusalem, the holy city. The uncircumcised and defiled will not enter you again. Shake off your dust; rise up, sit enthroned, O Jerusalem. Free yourself from the chains on your neck, O captive Daughter of Zion." I believe this is a crucial word for every believer to hear. It's an urgent call for every person to awaken to his or her divine purpose. Each of us is valuable to God and to the Body of Christ. Are you fully awake to that role? Have you been awakened to your assignment?

Maybe you have experienced trials in your life and have opted to give up on God and His plan. If so, I want to encourage you that God is with you, and He has given you all the grace you need to rise up out of difficulty. So don't give up on your assignment. You are alive at this point in history for a specific reason. You are here for such a time as this!

> *But make sure that you don't get so absorbed and exhausted in taking care of all your day-by-day obligations that you lose track of the time and doze off, oblivious to God. The night is about over, dawn is about to break. Be up and awake to what God is doing! God is putting the finishing touches on the salvation work he began when we first believed. We can't afford to waste a minute, must not squander these precious daylight hours in frivolity and indulgence, in sleeping around and dissipation, in bickering and grabbing everything in sight. Get out of bed and get dressed! Don't loiter and linger, waiting until the very last minute. Dress yourselves in Christ, and be up and about!*
>
> Romans 13:11-14 MSG

A "Wake Up" Moment

Recently, I personally experienced a time in which I had to "wake up" in the midst of difficult circumstances. When my father, Pastor

Billy Joe Daugherty, passed away in November of 2009, it was one of the hardest things I have ever dealt with. He and my mom founded Victory Christian Center over thirty years ago, and I expected them both to be there for years to come.

My husband, Caleb, and I were living on the mission field in Asia, when we got news of my dad's declining health. They informed us that we needed to come home immediately. So we hurried back to the USA and within a few hours of our arriving, Dad went to be with Jesus at only 57 years old.

It was not easy. I was close to my dad and looked up to him in so many ways. But more importantly, he was my hero. After his passing, I had a lot of questions like, *Why did this happen and what am I supposed to do now?* In the natural, it would have been easy for me to curl up in depression and confusion, but thankfully God reminded me of the dream He had given me three months earlier. I knew He still had a plan for my life and assignments He has called me to fulfill on this earth.

Five days after my dad's funeral, Caleb and I were scheduled to fly back to Cambodia. We were hosting a Christmas gift giveaway outreach for hundreds of children in remote villages, as well as hosting a women's conference, building water wells and finishing a church building project we had started.

At that time, I didn't feel like going or that I had much hope to offer, so I debated on whether to go or just stay home. But my mom reminded me of Jesus' example in Mark 6, when He heard that His cousin, John the Baptist, had been beheaded. It says that Jesus was grieved at the news and went to find a solitary place across the water. But when He got to the other side, there were multitudes of people waiting to hear from Him.

And Jesus saw a great multitude and was moved with COMPAS-SION for them, because they were like sheep not having a shepherd. So He began to teach them many things.

Mark 6:34 NKJV

After Jesus taught, the people were hungry. Jesus told His disciples to get them something to eat, but all they could find was a little boy with a small lunch of five loaves and two fish. He offered what he had to Jesus—and Jesus blessed it. That day, this little boy's lunch was supernaturally multiplied to feed over 5,000 people!

After sharing that story with me, my mom said, "Sarah, I believe if you will go in the midst of your own pain and loss, offer what is in your hand and just love the precious people of Cambodia, Jesus will do miracles." God is *so* faithful. That is exactly what happened. People were saved and healed by the power of God.

Hundreds of Christmas gift bags full of toys and practical items were given to children in the surrounding villages, thousands of pounds of food were given to families, hundreds of women were reached and blessed with practical gifts in the women's conference, a church was built, five water wells were completed, and resources were provided to expand the girls rescue home, which was built for those who had previously been enslaved in the sex trafficking industry. This was all truly done by the grace of God.

Not only was God faithful in helping me begin to fulfill the vision He had given me, but He also helped me expand it. While in the girls rescue home during that trip, I was so moved by the stories of what the girls had been through. One of the girls was sold by her godmother, and every time she escaped to go back to her, she would be sold again. She was sold to three brothels and was beaten terribly. When she was found in the street, she was so depressed that she was ready to end her life. But instead, she was rescued and brought to the girls home.

She wept as she shared with us how grateful she was for the love of God and the safe home she now lives in. Today, all of the girls are being trained in different trades, so when they graduate they can go back into society and live a normal life. Before we left, the girls sang us this song that has also become their anthem:

God has changed my name
I am no longer called
Wounded, outcast
Lonely or afraid
God has changed my name
My new name is
Confidence, joyfulness
Overcoming one
Faithfulness, friend of God
One who seeks God's face.

Jesus gives beauty for ashes. He truly is the God of new beginnings. Seeing these girls set free and beginning to understand their value brought an awakening in my heart.

Another night on this same trip, I walked into one of the churches and saw about 30 orphans sleeping on the floor. I asked the pastor about the kids and what we could do for them. Then God reminded me of a vision He had given me in a children's church worship service when I was 11 years old.

In the vision, I was standing with Jesus in front of a huge video screen. Suddenly, pictures of children from all over the world began to flash on the screen. They were hungry, alone, and hopeless. I asked Jesus, "Why are You showing me this?" He replied, "Because these are the people I have called you to reach."

When God reminded me of this vision, I knew I had to do something about what I had just seen. So I wrote out the plans to build an orphanage and began to share it. In ten days, all the funds came in to build the Hope for Children Home. Now 36 children are living in the orphanage. They are all being educated in both the school and in the Bible school. They have beds, clothes, shoes, schoolbooks, food, and clean drinking water. And this all happened because of the grace of God and people who caught onto His vision for the children.

Sometimes we can only see the pain right in front of us and feel like giving up. But if we will press through and fix our eyes on Jesus, He will give us strength to wake up and rise up. He will remind us that there are always *people* on the other side of our obedience. "Don't waste your time on useless work, mere busywork, the barren pursuits of darkness...Wake up from your sleep...Christ will show you the light! So watch your step. Use your head. Make the most of every chance you get. These are desperate times! Don't live carelessly, unthinkingly.

Make sure you understand what the Master wants" (Ephesians 5:14-17 MSG).

As we begin to wake up to God's purpose for our lives, we will quickly find that His purposes are "others-centered." In other words, they revolve around people. As we fulfill God's plan for our lives, we will draw others closer to Him.

It's time to wake up...
Out of Fear and into FAITH.
Out of Discouragement and into HOPE.
Out of Guilt and into FREEDOM.
Out of Worry and into PEACE.
Out of Distractions and into PURPOSE.
Out of Selfishness and into LOVE.
Out of Bitterness and into FORGIVENESS.
Out of Comparison and into Knowing your IDENTITY IN CHRIST.
Out of Weariness and into GOD'S STRENGTH.

2

RISE UP

When Caleb decided to propose to me about 11 years ago, he took me up in a helicopter over my hometown of Tulsa, Oklahoma. Since I knew he was the one for me and was ready for him to ask me to marry him, I immediately said *yes!*

As we were enjoying our helicopter ride over the city, I realized that things looked much different from that perspective than on the ground. I had grown up in Tulsa and lived there most of my life, but I had never seen the city from that perspective before. While driving on the road I could only see a mile or so ahead, but when I got up in the helicopter I could see the big picture—the whole layout of the city of Tulsa.

After that night, I thought about that experience in relation to my own life. I thought about how easy it is to get caught up in just thinking about the natural, temporal things, that we don't see the "big picture" that God has for our lives. Trust God that He has great things in store for you.

When we RISE UP and begin to understand who we are in Christ, we start to see our lives from a much different perspective. We realize that God has a divine purpose and assignment for us that is beyond our imagination. God has prepared great things for us to walk in. It's time to arise! *"Arise* [from the depression and prostration in which circumstances have kept you—rise to a new life]! Shine (be radiant with the glory of the Lord), for your light has come, and the glory of the Lord has risen upon you! For behold, darkness shall cover the earth, and dense darkness [all] peoples, but the Lord shall arise upon you ...and His glory shall be seen on you. And nations shall come to your light, and kings to the brightness of your rising" (Isaiah 60:1-3 AMP).

Arise means to get up, as from a sitting position, to awaken, to move upward. You may be in a place where you feel beaten down by circumstances and depression, but God is calling you to rise to a new life. He has a beautiful purpose for your life.

My grandmother, who has given me such a godly heritage, really struggled when my grandfather passed away. During that time, my dad spoke to her and said, "Mom, you can either sit in your rocking chair the rest of your life grieving over Dad, or you can get out and begin to help someone else." It was a strong statement, but it put things in perspective for her.

The next week, she began going to the nursing homes to visit people, praying for and encouraging them. She said she rose up out of that depression because she began to give out of herself to help others. *The Message* translation of Isaiah 60:1-3 says it this way, "Get out of bed, Jerusalem! Wake up. Put your face in the sunlight. God's bright glory has risen for you. The whole earth is wrapped in darkness, all people sunk in deep darkness, but God rises on you, his sunrise glory breaks over you. Nations will come to your light, kings to your sunburst brightness."

We must realize the times we are living in and wake up to the purpose God has for our lives. It is time to arise out of fear, complacency, and depression, and understand what God's will is for our lives. God has called us to SHINE! When we shine, people will be drawn to the light.

Born to Soar

There is an old story about a man who was visiting a farmer and was surprised to see a beautiful eagle in the farmer's chicken coop. "Why in the world have you got this eagle living in with the chickens?" the man asked.

"Well, I found him when he was little and raised him in there with the chickens. He doesn't know any better. He thinks he is a chicken," the farmer answered.

The man was dumbfounded. The eagle was pecking the grain and drinking from the watering can. The eagle kept his eyes on the ground and strutted around in circles, looking every inch like a big, over-sized chicken.

"Doesn't he ever try to spread his wings and fly out of there?" the man asked.

"No, and I doubt he ever will. He doesn't know what it means to fly," the farmer answered.

"Well, let me take him out and do a few experiments with him," the man said.

The farmer agreed, but assured the man that he was wasting his time. The man lifted the bird to the top of the chicken coop fence and said, "Fly!" He pushed the reluctant bird off the fence and it fell to the ground in a pile of dusty feathers. Next, the man took the ruffled chicken/eagle to the farmer's hayloft and spread its wings before tossing it high in the air again, yelling, "FLY!"

The frightened bird shrieked and fell ungraciously in the barnyard, where it resumed pecking the ground in search of dinner. Again, the man picked up the eagle and decided to give it one more chance, in a more appropriate environment away from the bad example of a chicken's lifestyle. He set the docile bird next to him on the front seat of his pickup truck and headed for the highest cliff in the country.

After a lengthy, sweaty climb to the crest of the cliff with the bird tucked under his arm, he spoke gently to the golden bird. "Friend, you were born to soar. It is better that you die here today on the rocks below than live the rest of your life being a chicken in a pen," he said.

Having said these final words, he lifted the eagle up and once more commanded it to "FLY!" He tossed the bird out into space and this time, much to his relief, it opened its seven-foot wingspan and flew gracefully into the sky. It slowly climbed in spirals into the glare of the morning sun. As crazy as this eagle sounds for not recognizing its true identity, we often do the same thing when we allow others to define our value, simply accepting the label they put on us.

Don't be like the eagle and allow others to define your self-worth or value. You were created by God. You are His masterpiece. You are seated with Christ. You are a child of the King. You have a divine assignment on earth—a holy purpose. "God raised us up with Christ and seated us with him in heavenly realms in Christ Jesus, in order that in the coming ages he might show the incomparable riches of his grace, expressed in his kindness to us in Christ Jesus" (Ephesians 2:6-7 NIV). He has called you to rise up and soar above the problems and fears of this world.

Understanding Your Value

If I took a $100 bill and crumpled it up, stomped on it and threw it in the trash, would it still be worth $100? YES, of course! If it wasn't completely destroyed, you could still go out and buy something with it. In life, many people have been stepped on, abused, and rejected. Consequently, they assume they have no value. But they are still valuable to God. He paid a great price for all of us—His own Son's life. (1 Peter 1:18-19).

Some people judge others by their outward appearance. Others judge them by their education, talent, achievements, or success. But this is the way the world looks at others, not the way God judges a person's value. The Bible says in 2 Corinthians 10:12 that it's not wise to compare yourself with others. God made you unique for a unique purpose.

I like the way John Mason puts it. He says, "You were born an original. Don't die a copy." The world portrays images of what a man or woman should be. If you look at magazines, TV, or movies, you can see how society tells us how we should look, dress, and talk. Although it is good to try to look our best, the Bible gives us a higher perspective of where our true value lies. "'For I know the plans I have for you' declares the LORD, 'plans to prosper you and not to harm you, plans to give you hope and a future. Then you will call upon me...and I will listen to you. You will seek me and find me when you seek me with all your heart'" (Jeremiah 29:11-13 NIV).

The key to understanding our value and purpose is to seek God first. For example, if you are a parent and have ever bought a large toy that came with many parts to assemble, you understand the importance of following the instruction manual step-by-step, in order to put it together correctly. I know from experience that when I try to put something together without looking at the manual, I usually mess it up or fail to understand the full function of the item.

Likewise, in our walk with God, in order for us to know our purpose on this earth, we must go back to the instruction manual of our Creator. God is our Creator and His Word is our instruction manual for life. He created us to do great things. "For we are God's workmanship, created in Christ Jesus to do good works, which God prepared in advance for us to do" (Ephesians 2:10 NIV).

Joyce Meyer tells how her father sexually abused her 200 times, when she was a young girl until she was 18 years old. She grew up in fear and shame, not knowing her true value. But as she got into God's Word, she began to understand God's love for her and received healing and restoration in her heart. She began to understand that God had a purpose for her life. She renewed her mind with the Word of God. Now she is on television every day, preaching the Gospel all over the world and sharing the life changing power of God's Word.

Katie Luce co-founded Teen Mania Ministries with her husband, Ron. Teen Mania is a youth ministry that reaches millions of young people through conferences. In her book, *The Pursuit of Beauty*, Katie talks about her struggle with understanding her identity and value. She struggled with an eating disorder in college, but when she began to meditate on who God said she was, she broke free from that stronghold. Katie says the only way she got free was by getting into the Word of God and finding out what it said about her. Now she has risen up and shared her testimony to many other young women.

Psalm 139 says that God knew you in your mother's womb. He made you, and His thoughts of you are more than the grains of sand. He knows every hair on your head. So don't compare yourself with others. God made you unique for a purpose. He put specific gifts and talents on the inside of you.

There is a well-known worship leader and songwriter in the United States, Israel Houghton. Israel leads worship for Lakewood Church, the largest church in America. He was conceived out of wedlock and his father wasn't around much. His mother was told to have an abortion, but she decided to have the baby anyway. When Israel was born, he was taken from his mother because of the drugs in her system. Then someone came and encouraged her not to give up and she gave her life to Jesus.

Israel said in his book, *A Deeper Level*, that for a long time, he bought into the belief that he was an accident or mistake.*[1] But the more time he spent in God's presence, the more he began to understand the truth of Psalm 139. He came to the point that he realized God had a purpose for his life. He began to pursue music and songwriting. Today, his music is heard all over the world. One of his songs impacts many people around the world with these simple, yet profound words, *I have a Maker, ...He knows my name.*

You are not a mistake. You are not an accident. The circumstances surrounding your birth may not have been ideal, but God meant for you to be here. God knows you by name. He knows how many hairs are on your head. He cares about you and has a great purpose for your life. In fact, 1 Corinthians 2:9-10 in the Message Bible says that what God has arranged for you is beyond your imagination, but He promises to reveal that purpose to you by His Spirit.

Another man, James Robinson, has a worldwide TV ministry that also touches millions of people. He was born, as what some would consider a "mistake," because his mother was raped. But God still had a plan for his life. Today his ministry feeds millions of hungry children in Africa because he chose to believe God had a purpose for his life.

You have been chosen by God. "You are a chosen people, a royal priesthood, a holy nation, a people belonging to God, that you may declare the praises of him who called you out of darkness into his wonderful light" (1 Peter 2:9 NIV). You are a royal child of the King. You are called to declare His praises. And you can make a difference in the lives of others.

So why did God make you the way you are? Why are you here at this time in history? You are here now, just the way you are, because God knew the world would need you. You have talents and abilities the world needs. When you realize God loves you and has a purpose for your life, your life will take on a whole new meaning. You are called to make a difference in the lives of others, no matter where you live or work.

My family knew a man named Benson Idahosa. He was born sickly in Nigeria, West Africa. His father didn't want another mouth to feed, so he told Benson's mother to throw the baby out. She wrapped Benson in a blanket and threw him into the trash heap. They thought he was dead. But later that evening, it began to rain and Benson began to cry. His mother heard him, rescued him, and hid him from his father.

Benson grew up very poor. He never even had a pair of shoes until he was 17 years old. But God saw his worth. When he was 17 years old, he received Jesus Christ as His Lord and Savior and believed God called him into ministry. He began to do outreaches village by village before establishing his church in Benin City. By 1971, he had established churches all over Nigeria and Ghana. He started Christian schools, a Bible institute, a Christian university and even a hospital in his city. During his lifetime, he shared the gospel in 148 nations of the earth. Even though he has now gone on to be with the Lord, his legacy lives on. He made a difference because he got a revelation that God loved him and he was valuable.

You may feel worthless or insignificant, but God values you. He gave His life for you to be saved and restored. He has a purpose for your life that involves helping others with His love. God wants to reveal to you that He gave His life for you and has created you for a divine purpose.

I met a woman from Nepal who grew up with a very hard life, and because of her hardship she became overwhelmed with depression and struggled with thoughts of suicide. But one day, she called out to God for help and He began to reveal His love for her. She received hope that He had a good plan for her life. She chose to rise up out of depression and get into God's Word. As she did, she started to realize she could help others rise up out of depression and abuse, as well. Now, she and her husband pastor a church in Nepal. They have also established a rescue home for girls coming out of sex trafficking, as well as a boys' home for those living on the streets. They are training these young people to be leaders in their nation.

One of the best examples in the Bible of someone who rose up to make a difference is Esther. Esther was both an orphan and a Jew. Even though the Jews were considered outcasts in Persia, God elevated her to be the Queen of Persia. She was put in a position where she could make a difference. During that time, a decree went out for all the Jews to be killed. Her Uncle Mordecai sent word to her, "Do not think in your heart that you will escape in the king's palace any more than all the other Jews. For if you remain completely silent at this time, relief and deliverance will arise for the Jews from another place, but you and your father's house will perish. Yet who knows whether you have come to the kingdom for such a time as this?" (Esther 4:13-14 NKJV).

At first, Esther was afraid to say anything because she knew if she went before the king unannounced, she could be executed. But when she heard that word from Mordecai, she *awakened* to her purpose. She realized that she had a responsibility to speak up for her people. She fasted and prayed for God's wisdom and favor.

God gave her the strategy to communicate to the king. So she rose up with courage, went before the king and invited him and Haman to a special banquet she prepared for them. When it came time for her to share with the king, she told him of Haman's plot to kill all the Jews, which included her and her family. The king was outraged. He ordered that Haman be executed.

The Jews were saved because Esther got out of her self-centeredness and fear. She realized she was not in the position of queen just to look pretty or have a title, but she was in that position to make a difference in the lives of others for God's glory. Just like Esther, you are called for a royal purpose. "As He is so are we in this world" (I John 4:17 NKJV). You are His witnesses. It's time to rise up to your divine assignment in the earth.

Freely Receive; Freely Give

After I had the vision I explained earlier, and began to recognize my call to the nations at age 12, I decided to go on my first mission trip to Mexico with a group of young people from our church. I remember seeing children living in trash dumps and it rocked my world. I realized how blessed we are, and compassion exploded in my heart to want to bless those in need.

When I came home, my dad encouraged me to find a regular place in the church where I could serve. As the pastor of our church, my dad knew we needed to share with others the love and wisdom from God's Word that we were receiving. "...Freely you have received, freely give" (Matthew 10:8 NKJV). I needed to *arise* out of selfishness and begin to give out on a regular basis.

I made a decision to get out of my comfort zone and get involved helping in our children's bus ministry service that bussed in hundreds of children from government-subsidized apartment complexes. As I was involved in loving on these precious children, compassion grew in my heart for those who were lost and without hope.

Throughout the years, I was involved in different areas of the church serving. I believe by giving out on a regular basis, not only was I able to help others, but my life was enriched as well. I have found that the only way to keep the fire of God in my life is to spend time with Jesus on a daily basis through prayer and the Word, and give out to others what I receive on a regular basis. I believe we grow when we give out of ourselves. Our heart becomes enlarged as we serve others.

Call to the Nations

In August of 2007, God spoke to me in a time of worship at our church. A minister who we love and respect was scheduled to speak that night, and I came with such expectation to hear from God. I said, "Lord, I feel I have surrendered everything in my life that I know of, but if there is anything else I need to do, show me. I am Yours."

It was as if God was waiting for me to ask that question. He replied, "Would you be willing to sell your home and move your family to the mission field for a period of time?" Then He reminded me of another family in our church who had done this several years earlier. Since they were prepared to go, God sent them to the mission field in Russia and Europe when the doors were first opened to the Gospel. They planted Bible schools in many nations that were ripe for the Gospel.

At that time in our lives, we were the young adult pastors at our church and the directors of teen mission outreaches. We loved serving under our pastors—my parents. We also loved the young people we had the privilege to work with at the church. I was seven months pregnant with our second child, Elizabeth, and Isaac was 2 1/2 years old.

I had been on many short-term mission trips, but I had not planned on living overseas at this time. I was comfortable working in our home church in the States, but God told me that if we didn't step out in faith and obedience to what He was saying, we would stagnate in our walk with Him and hinder the future growth of the young adults program we were leading.

We had started the young adult service at our church five years ago with about twenty people, and it had grown to include several hundred young adults on a weekly basis. We knew this was the result of the grace of God on our lives during that season. But now God was speaking to us to step out in a new direction to reach the nations.

When I heard God speak this to me, I surrendered and said, "Yes, Lord, but You will have to tell my husband, to confirm that this is of You." I did not know this at the time, but God had already spoken to

Caleb a few weeks earlier, while he was on a mission trip to Cambodia and Hong Kong.

He was in Cambodia helping to host an outreach, and while in Hong Kong on his way back home, God asked him the same question He asked me. He asked, "Would you be willing to move to this part of the world for the next season of your life?" Caleb said, "Yes Lord, but you will have to speak to my wife."

When Caleb came home from that trip, he didn't tell me what God had said to him. But that evening when I told him what God had spoken to me, he began to weep. He told me that God had already been showing him how we were called to go into nations throughout Asia, specifically Hong Kong and Cambodia.

That night, we made the decision together as a couple and said, "Yes, Lord, here we are. Send us." We had to rise up out of fear and out of our comfort zone and determine that we were going to let our light shine in the nations to which He had called us. "Go into all the world and preach the good news to all creation. Whoever believes and is baptized will be saved, but whoever does not believe will be condemned. And these signs will accompany those who believe: In my name they will drive out demons; they will speak in new tongues.... they will place their hands on sick people and they will get well" (Mark 16:15-18 NIV).

As David Livingstone, a well-known missionary to Africa, said, "If a commission by an earthly king is considered an honor, how can a commission by a Heavenly King be considered a sacrifice?" During that time of praying and seeking the Lord, God began to give us wisdom and divine appointments with people He wanted us to connect with. He began to give us His strategy for what He wanted us to do. He reminded us of the dreams and visions He had put in each of our hearts many years before.

We had been faithful to do what God had called us to do, and now He was releasing us to step out into something new. But just because we knew God was leading us to step out, did not mean that everyone understood us or agreed with our decision. Some people, even those in the church, thought we were a little crazy for quitting our wonderful jobs, selling our home and car, and moving a 1-year-old and 3-year-old to another country.

We had, what you would call, the "American Dream." We were grateful for what God had provided for us, but we still knew He had spoken to us and our obedience to Him would open up doors to reach more people than we could ever imagine. The time period from when God spoke to us to when we were scheduled to move really challenged our faith. We had to go through a process of dying to ourselves and completely trusting God. We first shared what God had told us with my parents and our pastors, and then other spiritual leaders.

When we told my parents, even though they wanted us to obey God's voice, it was still hard for them to let go of their children and grandchildren, not knowing when we would return. They also had lots of questions, just like any loving parents would. I remember sitting in my car after a conversation with them, crying and thinking about leaving, when a song rose in my heart and I began to sing to the Lord, *I will take up my cross and follow Your will. I lay down my life.* Then the

Lord brought to my remembrance Matthew 10:37,39: "Anyone who loves his father or mother more than me is not worthy of me; anyone who loves his son or daughter more than me is not worthy of me. Whoever finds his life will lose it, and whoever loses his life for my sake will find it."

Jim Elliot, a missionary who gave his life in the 1950s to reach the Inca Indians in Ecuador, said "He is no fool who gives up what he cannot keep, to gain that which he cannot lose." So we surrendered our lives to God and began to take the steps He told us to take. He supernaturally helped us sell our home in two weeks, during a time when the housing market was down.

There were many times when God spoke to us, telling us to give sacrificially to different people and church projects. It didn't make sense in the natural because we needed funds in order to move. But we realized that what we had in our hand was not enough for the dream God had put in our hearts, and that if we would place it in God's hands as a seed, He could multiply it. That was a test of our faith, but God proved Himself faithful and began to bring provision in ways we never would have imagined.

Once we moved, God began to open up doors that we couldn't open on our own. He connected us with a wonderful church family and friends overseas and opened up doors of opportunity to reach people throughout that region. God has a supernatural global positioning system for His people, and He will direct us if we take the time to tune into His voice and be willing to obey what He says.

I love what William Carey, the father of modern missions, said, "To know the will of God we need an open Bible and an open map."

3

THE GREATEST TREASURE

A certain old recluse lived deep in the mountains of Colorado. When he died, distant relatives came from the city to collect his valuables. But upon arriving, all they saw was an old shack with an outhouse beside it.

Inside the shack, next to the rock fireplace was an old cooking pot and the man's mining equipment. A cracked table with a three-legged chair stood guard by the tiny window, and a kerosene lamp served as the centerpiece for the table. In a dark corner of the little room was a dilapidated cot with a threadbare bedroll on it.

The relatives picked up some of the old relics and started to leave. As they were driving away, an old friend of the recluse, riding on his mule, flagged them down. "Do you mind if I help myself to what's left in my friend's cabin?" he asked.

"Go right ahead," they replied. After all they thought, "What inside that shack could be worth anything?"

The old friend entered the shack and walked directly over to the table. He reached under it and lifted one of the floor boards. Then he took out all the gold his friend had discovered over the past fifty-three years. It was enough to build a palace!

The recluse died with only his friend knowing his true worth. As the friend looked out of the little window and watched the cloud of dust behind the relative's car disappear, he said, "They should've gotten to know him better."[2]

There are many people who miss out on a lot of wonderful things God has for them, because they don't understand the treasure they have in Him. They don't take the time to get to know Him in a personal way. God has so much in store for us. But we must take the time to get to know Him. Much like the relatives in the story, we can miss out on the "gold" of God by not taking the time to know Him.

I grew up in church and was saved at a young age. However, I didn't realize that Jesus wanted to have a personal relationship with me until I was 14 years old and had an encounter with Him during a time of worship at a youth camp. I heard Jesus ask me, "Sarah, am I first in your life?" I thought, *Yeah, I am a good girl, and I am saved.* Then He asked, "Sarah, am I your best friend?"

I realized then that I was saved and knew about the Bible but didn't really have a close relationship with God. I wasn't seeking to know Him as a friend. I cared more about what my peers thought about me than about developing my relationship with God. That night, I was awakened to my spiritual condition and surrendered my all to Jesus. I made a decision to seek Him to know Him more. "Then you will call upon me and come and pray to me, and I will listen to you.

You will seek me and find me when you seek me with all your heart" (Jeremiah 29:12-13 NIV).

That night, I completely prostrated myself on the chapel floor, worshiping Him and listening to what He had to say about my life. After that experience, I decided to get up early each day to spend time with God before school. At first, I started with 15 minutes, and then the time grew more each day. I got a devotional book to help me learn how to spend time with God. I began to learn how to study the Word, meditate on it, pray, hear His voice, and be led by His Spirit. God became real to me, and I began to realize the *treasure* it was to know Jesus.

During that season, my friendships changed because the people I had been hanging out with were focused on other things, and we didn't seem to relate anymore. Even though at that time, it seemed like I had lost my close friends, God was doing something in me. He was drawing me to seek Him first. "Seek first the kingdom of God...and all these things shall be added you" (Matthew 6:33 NKJV).

Over time, God brought me friends who were passionate for Him and would sharpen me in my walk with Him. But He still wanted to remain number one. As we fix our eyes on God, we will find treasures waiting to be discovered.

There was a young man named Jason, who was about to graduate from high school. He came from a wealthy family and was expecting to get a new car from his parents for graduation. Jason and his father had spent months looking at cars, and the week before graduation they found the perfect one. Jason felt certain this car would be his on graduation night.

Imagine his disappointment, when immediately following the graduation ceremony, his father handed him a small elegantly wrapped package. *It must be the keys to my new car,* Jason thought. But upon opening the gift, all he found was a Bible with his name imprinted on the front. *A Bible,* he thought. He took it out, looking to find the car keys in the box. But it was empty.

Jason was so angry—throwing the Bible down, he stormed out of the house. His father tried to stop him and explain, but Jason kept running. He never saw his father again. News of his father's death finally brought him home again.

As Jason went through the possessions he was about to inherit from his father, he came across the graduation Bible. Brushing away the dust, he opened it and began idly flipping through the pages. A paper tucked inside caught his eye, so he pulled it out. It was a cashier's check, dated the day of his graduation for the exact amount to pay for the car he and his father had chosen. What was his father trying to tell him? His father wanted him to see the importance of seeking God first, and that as he did that, God would give him the desires of his heart.

Just like Jason's father, our Heavenly Father has placed treasures in His Word that He wants to reveal to us. "Good friend, take to heart what I'm telling you; collect my counsels and guard them with your life. Tune your ears to the world of Wisdom; set your heart on a life of Understanding. That's right—if you make Insight your priority and won't take no for an answer, Searching for it like a prospector panning for gold, like an adventurer on a treasure hunt, Believe me, before you know it Fear-of-GOD will be yours; you'll have come upon the Knowledge of God" (Proverbs 2:1-5 MSG). As you seek God, you will discover the amazing treasures in His Word, and in those treasures you will find the knowledge of God.

Tune In

God desires to speak to you and guide you in the big, as well as in the little things of life. But you must take time to tune into His voice, just as if you were to turn a radio on and try to tune into a specific station. In order to get to the station you want, you have to get past the static and other channels and hone into the one you want to hear.

In life there are many voices vying for our attention—our job, family, friends, music, TV, phone, social media, etc. Some of the voices around us can be good, but some can totally distract us from the plan God has for our lives. The most important voice we should be tuning into is God's voice, because He knows the plans He has for us and the steps we need to take to get there.

Our environment can have so much noise that it can even hinder us from even hearing God's voice. It is vital for us to realize that we have to get in an environment where we can quiet our hearts, get in God's Word, and say, "Lord, I want Your wisdom more than human intellect or anything else, I want to know Your wisdom because I know it will help me in everything that I do."

The way we begin to recognize His voice is by spending time with Him, just like we get to know others by spending time with them. When my husband calls me, he doesn't have to introduce himself. I know his voice immediately because we have spent time together. That's how it is with God's Word and His presence. When we spend time with God, we begin to learn His voice and hear from Him throughout our whole day. He will guide us in the big and little things in life.

The Bible calls us God's sheep because we are His children. "My sheep hear My voice" (John 10:27 NKJV). The first and foremost way we hear the voice of God is through His Word. "In the beginning was the Word, and the Word was with God, and the Word was God" (John 1:1 NKJV). If we want to know Jesus, we have to seek out the Word. There's a tendency to get so busy with life that we neglect to do this, but I want you to recognize the vital importance of making the Word your first priority.

If you will seek God's wisdom, He will add everything else you need. He will add the right spouse to you. He will add the right job and provision you need. He will add the grace and wisdom you need in raising your children. As you seek His wisdom, He will guide you into the assignment He has for your life. His Word is full of promises for those who seek Him.

A Personal GPS System

I will admit that I am the kind of person who needs help with directions when I drive. One night, I was going with a group of girls to a party that our young adult church group was hosting. The house we were going to was on the other side of town, and I did not have a clue where we were going. I could just imagine getting lost somewhere out in the country (since that has happened to me before).

After driving in the dark a while, one of the girls pulled out her iPhone and exclaimed, "Oh, I have GPS on my phone, it will get us there in no time!" Sure enough, she typed in the address and it told us exactly which turns to take. We even got there on time.

God's Word is like a GPS system. It's a positioning system for direction and wisdom for the things we're supposed to do. Just like with a GPS, we can get so lost without it. We can get on crazy detours, if we're not in tune to His wisdom.

You might know people like that—who just got off on a wrong detour in their life because they neglected the Word of Wisdom. They made one wrong decision and it caused their whole life to spiral off track. "...(God's Word will) keep you from making wrong turns, or following bad directions…" (Proverbs 2:12 MSG). Or perhaps, you have taken a detour but are now trying to get back on God's path. If so, I want to encourage you not to be condemned by the past. Just repent and jump on God's plan.

Get back on the road and begin to pursue God and His wisdom. He will take care of the rest. He will restore you and give you wisdom for your future. Don't live in condemnation, fear, or worry. If you trust in Him and pursue His Word, you will have divine grace and guidance for the things that He has called you to do.

The Light of God's Word

God's Word is also like a light. Without it, we are in darkness. In Psalm 119:105 NKJV, David declares to God "Your word is a lamp to my feet and a light to my path." The Message translation of that same passage says, "By your words I can see where I'm going, they throw a beam of light on my dark path." That means God gives us direction for each step He wants us to take on a daily basis. Not only that, but He is also a light to our path. In other words, His Word is a light to our long-range plans and He will give us direction for our future. "The entrance of Your words gives light, it gives understanding to the simple" (Psalm 119:130).

In this day and age, we need the wisdom of God like never before. We cannot only rely on human wisdom or man's intellect; we need supernatural revelation knowledge to live the life that God has called us to live in order to fulfill His purpose.

Every day, we constantly make decisions that will chart the course for the rest of our lives. We make decisions on where we will go to school, what career we will choose, where we will work, who we will date, who we will marry, when we will get married, etc.... With all these questions going through our mind, we need the wisdom of God like never before so we don't get off on a detour.

We need to stay on the path that God has planned for and destined us to walk in. "...in all your ways, acknowledge him and he will make your paths straight" (Proverbs 3:6 NIV). In all of our days we should acknowledge Him. God has a purpose for every single day and He says if we will put Him first in each one, He will direct our path.

We all need direction in one area or another in our lives. We might say, "Well, okay, but in the Bible, it doesn't really say the name of the person I should marry or exactly which job I am to take." But as you get to know Jesus by spending time in His Word, you will also begin to know His will, His ways, and His character. You will learn His voice and the Holy Spirit will say, "This is the way. Walk in it." He will give you direction concerning the person you will marry or the school you will attend. You may not see these things plainly in His Word, but God promises that if we seek wisdom, He will direct us.

Awakened to Hear

He wakens me morning by morning, wakens my ear to listen like one being taught. The Sovereign LORD has opened my ears, and I have not been rebellious; I have not drawn back.

Isaiah 50:4-5 NIV

When the alarm goes off in the morning, and I wake my kids up for school, one of the first things they ask for is food. My seven year-old son Isaac is a growing boy, and he especially loves a big breakfast with eggs, bacon, waffles, cereal, and fruit. On the other hand, my daughter Elizabeth isn't always hungry, but I still make sure she eats something because I know she needs nourishment. As a mom, I want to make sure my children have the energy they need to face the day.

In the same way, I believe our Heavenly Father is awakening us to seek Him first for the nourishment we need for each new day. If we seek Him first, we will find the assignment and plan He has for our lives. God's Word is like food for our spirit man. In fact, Jesus called

Himself the *Bread of Life*. The bread people ate in Bible days was considered the main course of a meal. Basically, Jesus was saying that He is the *main* thing. He is the source of life. "I am the bread of life. He who comes to Me shall never hunger, and he who believes in Me shall never thirst" (John 6:35 NKJV).

In Exodus 16, when the children of Israel were in the wilderness, God supernaturally rained manna (bread) down from heaven each day. They were instructed not to take more than they needed for that day or else it would spoil. God asked the Israelites to trust Him for their provision and nourishment every single day.

In the same way, I believe God has fresh "manna" or spiritual food for us each day—a fresh word to strengthen and direct us. We must seek Him as our source of life daily. "Like newborn babies you should crave (thirst for, earnestly desire) the pure (unadulterated) spiritual milk, that by it you may be nurtured and grow into [completed] salvation" (I Peter 2:2 AMP).

We must awaken our spirits to hunger and thirst after God's Word and His presence. As we seek Him and tune into His voice, we will discover many treasures.

4

ARMED AND DANGEROUS

When I first moved to Hong Kong, I decided to go out for a run around our apartment complex. As I was running, I turned a corner to find something I'd only seen in movies. Right in front of me was a Chinese woman with a huge Samurai sword pointing right at me! Immediately, I imagined the music in the background, *Everybody Was Kung Fu Fighting...*

As I stopped and looked around, I realized there wasn't just one woman—there was a whole group of them. They were on guard with their swords drawn, practicing a form of Chinese martial arts. Their eyes were serious, fixed and determined, and they were not about to move out of the way for me. As quickly as I could, I turned right around and ran in the other direction. That was my initiation to Asia.

Later, I thought back on that story and recognized its relevance to our lives as believers. The second statement in Isaiah 52:1 NIV says, "clothe yourself with strength." In the Message translation it says, "Pull on your boots," which symbolizes preparing to take action.

It is incredibly crucial for us to be aware that in this race of life we're running, the enemy will try to stop us. He will try to hold us back from fulfilling our destiny. And if we're not prepared, we may turn right around and give up on it. That's why God says we must put on our strength.

How do we put on our strength? Isaiah 40:31 says "Those who wait on the LORD (put their hope in, put their faith in the Lord) shall renew their strength. They shall mount up with wings like eagles, they shall run and not be weary, they shall walk and not faint" (NKJV, explanation mine). We put on our strength daily as we spend time meditating on God's Word, speaking it boldly, and lifting our praise and worship to Him.

The Place of Strength

That secret place of strength is found in God's presence. King David cried out to the Lord in Psalm 27:

> *"One thing I have desired of the LORD, That will I seek: That I may dwell in the house of the LORD all the days of my life... In the secret place of His tabernacle He shall hide me; He shall set me high up on a rock. When You said, 'Seek My face,' My heart said to You, 'Your face, LORD, I will seek.' I would have lost heart, unless I had believed that I would see the goodness of the LORD in the land of the living. Wait on the LORD, be of good courage, and He will strengthen your heart; Wait, I say, on the LORD".*

Psalm 27:4-5,8,13

To wait on the Lord means to put your hope in, look unto, and put your trust and faith in the Lord. When you wait upon Him, there's a time of sitting and waiting. You can do this throughout your day. You can put on faith and expectation in the Lord throughout anything you do or go through. Waiting on the Lord will strengthen your heart. "He gives power to the weak, and to those who have no might He increases strength. Even the youths shall faint and be weary, and the young men shall utterly fall, but those who wait on the LORD shall renew their strength, They shall mount up with wings like eagles, They shall run and not be weary, They shall walk and not faint" (Isaiah 40:29-32 NKJV).

Each of us faces weariness, but the Bible promises if we will make God our goal and desire every day, we will have renewed strength for the vision He has put in our heart. We will have strength to say *no* to temptation and to finish the things He's assigned us to do. But we need an infusion of His strength on a daily basis, and that comes as we wait upon Him.

Strengthen Your Core

After I had my first baby, Isaac, my body was weak from being stretched out over nine months of pregnancy (those of you who are moms understand this). I felt like my strength and energy was "zapped." I knew I needed to do something about it, but I wasn't sure how to get started or what to do.

One night, while I was up in the middle of the night feeding Isaac, I flipped on the TV. There was an infomercial talking about strengthening your "core." Your core or midsection is your "power-house"—where all your movements come from. They explained that strengthening your core would help you become more stable and stronger in all areas.

I realized what I needed in order to rebuild my strength and get back in shape was to focus on this area—my core. I may have been a little sleep deprived, but I ordered this exercise contraption to help strengthen my core anyway. However, once I received it, I realized it was not going to do a miracle for my body unless I was consistent in doing the exercises on a daily basis. The key to seeing the reward of a strong core was in the *consistency* of the workout.

This same principle can be applied to strengthening your spirit. You may feel like your spiritual energy is zapped and you don't have the strength to overcome temptations or fulfill the will of God for your life. Maybe it's been too long since you opened up your Bible or said a short prayer. Well, even more than strengthening your physical core, it's vital to strengthen your spiritual core—your heart and spirit. So how do you do that? You do it by meditating on the Word and speaking it out of your mouth.

Out of your heart flows the issues of life (Proverbs 4:23). Out of your heart flows your thoughts, your words, and your actions. When that tug-of-war comes into your mind and tries to allow negativity into your heart, begin to speak and meditate on the Word. It will strengthen you so that you can say *no* to those temptations. Like physical strengthening, this strengthening is a continual process, but you will see the reward of your decisions.

There is a reward for you as you consistently seek God, even when no one else is watching. When you're seeking Him, you're building up your spirit man, enabling you to overcome the attacks of the enemy. "When you pray, go into your room, and when you have shut your door, pray to your Father who is in the secret place; and your Father who sees in secret will reward you openly" (Matthew 6:6 NKJV).

Feed Your Faith

So how do we stay strong in faith? By feeding our faith regularly. In order for a plant to grow, it must be fed. It must get water and sunlight, the weeds must be pulled out, and the soil must be prepared properly so the plant can grow without limitations. Our faith is the same way. Each of us has been given a measure of faith like a mustard seed (Matthew 17:20). "Faith comes by hearing, and hearing by the Word of God" (Romans 10:17 NKJV). When we hear or read God's Word, it is like a seed that's planted in our heart. But if fear and doubt choke out that word, it will not grow (Matthew 13). We have to feed our faith in God on a regular basis by hearing the Word preached at church, as well as taking time to read and meditate on it each day. If we only hear the Word on Sunday, then many times during the week, the cares of life will overwhelm us. That is why we must feed on what God's Word says on a daily basis. We must not let the cares of this world come in and choke the Word from our heart.

As followers of God, we are called to live by faith (Hebrews 10:38). We receive everything from Him by faith. Salvation comes through faith in Jesus Christ (Romans 10:9-10). Healing comes through faith in Jesus (Luke 8:48; 1 Peter 2:24). In fact, Hebrews 6:12 says that we receive ALL the promises of God through faith and patience. We receive peace, joy, wisdom, and provision—all through faith in Jesus and His Word. Not only that, but Hebrews 11:6 NKJV says, "Without faith it is impossible to please Him, for he who comes to God must believe that He is, and that He is a rewarder of those who diligently seek Him." So, through faith we receive from God, and through faith we are pleasing to God.

Jonathan, one of the young men in our church, was diagnosed with cancer in his knee when he was 16 years old. He was a track star and had been offered a college scholarship. But the doctors said the cancer was so bad, they were going to have to amputate his knee. He and his family made a decision not to tell people the negative report, but instead they took two weeks to focus on prayer and speak the word of faith over his body. In fact, they began to call him *Jonathan New Knees.*

They filled their home with an environment of faith by playing healing scripture CD's and songs. They called me over, as one of Jonathan's youth pastors, to come and pray for him, but before I even got there, they made a decision to believe God for a miracle. After two weeks, they went to the doctor and he couldn't find the cancer. Jonathan was totally healed!

In God's Word, He has given us all the tools we need to overcome whatever challenges we may face.

Be strong in the Lord and in His mighty power. Put on the full armor of God so that you can take your stand against the devil's schemes. For our struggle is not against flesh and blood, but against the rulers...of this dark world and against the spiritual forces of evil in the heavenly realms. Therefore put on the full armor of God, so that when the day of evil comes, you may be able to stand your ground, and after you have done everything, to stand. Stand firm then, with the belt of truth buckled around your waist, with the breastplate of righteousness in place, and with your feet fitted with the readiness that comes from the gospel of peace. In addition to this, take up the shield of faith, with which you can extinguish all the flaming arrows of the evil one. Take the helmet of salvation and the sword of the Spirit, which is the word of God. And pray in the Spirit on all occasions with all kinds of prayers and requests.

Ephesians 6:10-18 NIV

We have been given all we need for life and godliness. The sword of the Spirit, which is described in Ephesians 6, is the spoken Word of God. It is our weapon against the lies of the enemy. But we must choose to "take it up" and lift up that shield of faith when attacks come our way.

There is power when we believe and speak God's Word with faith over our lives. This is the spirit of faith: we believe and therefore we speak (2 Corinthians 4:13). When we speak His Word in the midst of problems, we are taking up our sword and using our authority as a believer.

Our Fight of Faith for Our Son

In our family, Caleb and I have stood in faith for many things, but as a mom, one of the hardest things to stand for was my son Isaac's health. During our first flight to Hong Kong, he had a reaction to some shots he had been given and stopped breathing on the plane. He was given CPR and put on an oxygen tank. Finally, he started breathing but had another episode on the plane only a few hours later.

When we landed, we went straight to the doctor, and the next day Isaac was admitted to the hospital. He was very weak and after the medical tests, one doctor said he might have long-term effects from this incident. So Caleb and I began to pray and believe for a miracle.

The following week, we flew to Singapore and while we were there, Isaac had another episode. From Singapore, we were scheduled to fly to the Philippines. Fear tried to grip me, since I didn't know what might happen to Isaac if we traveled again. But we prayed and felt we were supposed to go.

That week in the Philippines, I remember being in the hotel room and feeling overwhelmed by fear, both about my son's health and about our move to the mission field. In that moment, the Lord spoke to my heart, "Sing, Sarah. Worship Me." I was tired and didn't feel like singing because the enemy was trying to sow lies of fear in my heart by saying, "Why are you here? Did you really hear from God that you are supposed to be here? You need to go home and give up."

But still, in that room all by myself, with tears streaming down my face, I began to sing.

As I sang, faith rose up in my heart and my focus shifted from my situation to the greatness of God. I got the victory in my heart. Immediately, I started speaking the Word over my son with faith. I declared that he was the healed of the Lord, and that by Jesus' stripes he was redeemed from the curse.

This reminded me of the story in 2 Chronicles 20:3, when King Jehoshaphat was facing an attack from the people of Moab and Ammon. It says that he feared only for a moment, and then he immediately set himself to seek God. God spoke to him in verse 15 saying, "The battle is not yours but mine!" Jehoshaphat sent the worshippers ahead of the army, and when they began to praise God, He sent ambushes against the people of Moab and Ammon and they were defeated. King Jehoshaphat faced an impossible situation, but instead of running in fear, he sought God in faith and God gave him direction. Worship is spiritual warfare.

During that time as I worshipped, faith rose up in my heart, and I began to speak the Word of God over Isaac. I began to take up my sword of the Spirit and boldly declare he was healed by the stripes of Jesus (1 Peter 2:24). I declared that he would live and not die to declare the works of the Lord. I spoke life, health, and strength over my son's body.

As I asked God for wisdom, He began to show me some natural things to do to also help Isaac recover quickly. As we stood in faith that week, Isaac regained strength and has never had a seizure since that day. We praise God that he is healthy and whole.

I believe praise is a powerful weapon against the enemy. Breakthroughs happen as we praise God. He can work a miracle in whatever situation we face regarding our health, finances, family, or career. But we must make a decision to live in faith, not in fear, and to speak what God's Word says instead of how we feel.

Maybe God has put dreams in your heart or has given you a vision for your future. If so, you must act in faith to get there. Do what God tells you to do. Continue to feed your faith by meditating on what His Word says, then act on your faith and you will see miracles happen. This is not a time for us to live in a spirit of fear but in His power, love, and with a sound mind. You are armed and dangerous to the enemy, so put on your strength and fight the good fight of faith.

5

SHAKE IT OFF

There's an old parable about a farmer who had a donkey that fell into a very deep pit. He assumed the donkey was dead and figured there was no way he could get him out of the pit, so he decided to fill in the hole to prevent further injuries to his other animals. Meanwhile, the confused, yet uninjured (and very much alive) donkey was trying to figure out what had just happened. He stood up in the bottom of the pit and felt a pile of dirt land harshly on his back.

The donkey panicked. He was about to be buried alive! But then he had an idea. He shook off the dirt. Almost immediately, another pile of dirt came down. Again, he shook it off. After a while, the donkey realized that he had shaken off enough dirt to form a pile below his feet, so he stepped up onto that pile. By the end of the night, the donkey had shaken off enough dirt that he was able to walk out of that pit unharmed.

That's what we are encouraged to do in the next part of Isaiah 52:1. It instructs us to shake off the dust. Obviously, we are not stuck in an actual pit, so what kind of dust is Isaiah referring to? He's talking about anything that keeps us from rising up and completing our assignment. Dust is something that keeps an object from shining. It can symbolize fear, doubt, or shame. You and I must shake off the lies of the enemy that keep us from shining in the midst of darkness.

Anytime we are on the path to fulfilling our assignment, there are many distractions that will try to keep us from completing it. That's because the enemy knows the potential that resides on the inside of us, and he will do anything he can to keep us in fear of stepping out into something greater. But we must wake up and realize that we are alive for "such a time as this." God has a purpose for us to fulfill so it's time to get up out of our pit, shake off the dust, and rise up as a light in this world.

Get Out of the Cave

In Judges 6, we find the story of a man named Gideon. Gideon was an Israelite and a cave dweller in both senses of the word. During this time, the children of Israel had drifted away from God. They began to worship other gods and got out from under God's protection. The Midianites (their enemies) took control for seven years, causing the Israelites to resort to dwelling in caves to hide from their enemies. Basically, the Israelites were living in a constant state of bondage and fear.

While Gideon was hiding in the cave, his eyes were opened to the promises that God had for him. The angel of the Lord brought a word that Gideon needed to hear: "And the Angel of the LORD appeared to him, and said to him, 'The LORD is with you, you mighty man of valor!'" (Judges 6:12 NKJV).

God was calling those things that are not as though they were (Romans 4:17 NIV). Gideon was not a strong, confident leader yet, and his reply demonstrated his fear. In Verse 13 he asked, "O my Lord, if the LORD is with us, why then has all this happened to us? And where are all His miracles which our fathers told us about . . .?" (NKJV).

God's reply was simple. He said, "Go in this might of yours, and you shall save Israel from the hand of the Midianites. Have I not sent you?" (v.14 NKJV). But Gideon proved his fear again by comparing himself with others. He asked, "But me? I'm the weakest. I'm the least. What do I have? Why are You choosing me, God?" (my paraphrase, v.15).

Comparison and doubt are both common distractions that we encounter on the road to fulfilling our destiny. It's easy to doubt God and think, *Well, if God is really with me, why are all these things happening to me?* But the truth is that we don't see the big picture like God does. We see a battle, but He sees a victory.

When we are tempted to get caught up in comparison, we need to remember that God won't help us become anyone else except the person He created us to be. Once Gideon shook off the lies of doubt and comparison, God began to use him greatly and he fulfilled his destiny. And the same can happen for us.

Maybe now you are beginning to recognize some of the dust you are dealing with. Maybe it's a fear of failure or shame from your past. Whatever it is, it's time to shake it off. How? By putting on your strength-- by renewing your mind through God's Word and taking every negative thought captive. "The weapons we fight with are not the weapons of the world. On the contrary, they have divine power to demolish strongholds. We demolish arguments and every pretension that sets itself up against the knowledge of God, and we take captive every thought to make it obedient to Christ" (2 Corinthians 10:4-5 NIV).

The devil's worst nightmare is that you and I are going to wake up and recognize our authority in Christ. He would love to keep us from fulfilling our dream and purpose by bringing thoughts of fear, comparison, and discouragement. So shake off the lies of the enemy and realize that Christ is in you.

God Is with You!

In Gideon's story in Judges 6:16 NKJV, the Lord said, "Surely I will be with you, and you shall defeat the Midianites as one man." He said something similar to Moses when he said, "I will certainly be with you" (Exodus 3:12 NKJV). If God is for you, no one can be against you. If He's got your back, you don't have to be afraid of what people will say or think, because He is with you. He will help you and give you the words to say. As Gideon was surrendered and obedient to God, the power of God came on him, and God began to use him. "...*the Spirit of the* LORD *came upon Gideon...*" (Judges 6:34 NKJV).

In the Old Testament, it talks about how the Spirit of the Lord came *upon* someone. But it's different in the New Testament, because for those who receive Christ, He promises to abide *in* us. We have the Spirit of God with us 24/7. We have something that Gideon didn't have because the Spirit of God is with us all the time, to guide us into all truth (John 16:13). "But you shall receive power when the Holy Spirit has come upon you; and you shall be witnesses to Me in

Jerusalem, and in all Judea and Samaria, and to the end of the earth" (Acts 1:8 NKJV). The power of the Holy Spirit is in us to empower us to fulfill God's assignment for our lives.

African Adventures

If we are fearful about a situation, it doesn't necessarily mean that God is not telling us to step out. In fact, many times when we are going forward in the things God has called us to do, we will feel some fear. But don't draw back. It takes courage to do what He has called you to do, no matter how you feel. Trust that God is with you.

When I was 16 years old, I went to Ghana, West Africa, with a teen group from our church. In the middle of the trip, our leaders divided us up into pairs and drove us to some of the remote northern villages. They told us we were going to spend the night with the people there and minister the next day at the church.

When we drove up to the village we were going to be staying in, I realized we were going to be spending the night in a mud and grass hut with no electricity, running water, or cell phones! I was with another 13-year-old girl who had never been on a mission trip before and a missionary's daughter who was 16 years old.

The three of us were in the middle of nowhere. On top of that, the pastor asked me to preach in their service the next day for an hour. I had never preached a whole sermon before. Immediately, I was wishing I had some of my dad's books to preach from, but all I had was my Bible. (I learned that day if all I have is the Bible, it is enough!)

That night as I was sleeping on the ground under my mosquito net, I prayed, *God, You have got to help me!* Suddenly, I heard bongo drums beating and people chanting outside. The witch doctor next door found out we were there, and he was not happy about it. Fear tried to grip me and imaginations came to my mind of all the things that might happen. I knew I had to take authority over those thoughts, so I started confessing, "God has not given me the spirit of fear but of power, love, and a sound mind" (2 Timothy 1:7).

When I began to fear what I was going to speak on the next day, the Holy Spirit reminded me of Jeremiah. When God called Jeremiah to be a mouthpiece for Him, Jeremiah said, "But, God, I cannot speak. I am just a youth." But God said, "Do not say, 'I am a youth,' for you shall go to all to whom I send you, and whatever I command you, you shall speak. Do not be afraid of their faces, for I am with you to deliver you," says the LORD" (Jeremiah 1:7-8 NKJV).

As I prayed that night, God began to show me the scriptures that the people needed to hear. I did not realize what this church had been facing, with the recent death of some of the church elders, but the words God gave me from Romans 8 were just what they needed to hear in order to be strengthened. Those words are just as powerful today as they were back then: "If God is for us, who can be against us? ...Who shall separate us from the love of Christ? Shall trouble or hardship or persecution or famine or nakedness or danger or sword? ...No, in all these things we are more than conquerors through him who loved us. For I am convinced that neither death nor life, neither angels or demons, neither the present nor the future, nor any powers, neither height nor depth, nor anything else in all creation, will be able to separate us from the love of God that is in Christ Jesus our Lord" (Romans 8:31, 35, 37-39 NIV).

This message brought hope to the people of the village that day, and people responded to the altar call with tears of joy. Even though I was young, I had to realize that if God called me to go there and speak to them, He would give me the words to say and would show up in power. God moved in a great way that weekend, and many were saved and healed. "Let no one despise your youth, but be an example to the believers in word, in conduct, in love, in spirit, in faith, in purity" (I Timothy 4:12 NKJV).

You may be young and say, "Well, maybe I'll do something for God when I am older, out of school, or when my children are grown." But I encourage you to start where you are today with what you have— your opportunities and talents—and do something for God. Don't be afraid. The longer you put off responding to the call of God, the more "unsure" you will become. This is the danger of procrastination— it brings doubt and uncertainty, which leads to disobedience and failure. Remember, God is for you, and you are more than a conqueror through Him.

Press Past Fear

Remember, David was only a teenager when he was used by God to kill a giant. All he had was a slingshot and five stones. This wasn't much compared to everyone else, but he didn't let fear or inadequacy keep him from killing the giant. He knew how big his God was, so he just shook off the dust.

When everyone else was hiding in fear, David defeated Goliath and fulfilled his assignment. So I encourage you, don't let anything hold you back from what God has called you to do. Be awake to what God is saying, put on your strength, shake off the lies of the enemy, and then run with confidence the race God has set before you. God is with you, and His power is greater than anything the enemy could ever try to bring against you. Shake off the dust!

6

FRESH AND
FLOURISHING

There is a story of an old man who lived high above an Austrian village along the slopes of the Alps. Many years ago, the town council hired this old man as "the keeper of the spring," to maintain the purity of the pools of water in the mountain crevices. The overflow from these pools of water ran down the mountainside and fed the lovely spring that flowed through the town.

Faithfully and quietly, the keeper of the spring patrolled the hills, removing the leaves and branches and wiping away the silt that would contaminate the fresh flow of water. As time went on, the village became a popular attraction for vacationers. The water was beautiful, and the farmlands were naturally irrigated.

Years passed. One evening the town council met for its semi-annual meeting. As the council members reviewed the budget, one man's eye caught the salary paid to the keeper of the spring. He asked, "Who is this old man? Why do we keep paying him year after year? No one ever sees him. For all we know, this man does us no good. He isn't necessary any longer."

By a unanimous vote, the council fired the man. For several weeks nothing changed. But by early autumn, the trees began to shed their leaves and small branches began to fall into the pools, hindering the flow of water. One afternoon, someone noticed a yellowish brown tint in the water. A few days later, it had darkened even more. The mill wheels finally stopped moving. Businesses near the water closed. Tourists no longer wanted to visit the town. Eventually, disease spread within the village.

Soon, the town council realized the importance of guarding the water source, so they hired the man back, and over a few weeks, the water was restored to its purity.[*1] Like the keeper of the spring, we are the keeper of our heart. What will help us stay fresh and flourishing every day? Keeping God's life consistently flowing through us and continually renewing our minds with His Word.

> So here's what I want you to do, God helping you: Take your everyday, ordinary life—your sleeping, eating, going-to-work, and walking-around life—and place it before God as an offering. Embracing what God does for you is the best thing you can do for him. Don't become so well-adjusted to your culture that you fit into it without even thinking. Instead, fix your attention on God. You'll be changed from the inside out. Readily recognize what he wants from you, and quickly respond to it. Unlike the culture around you, always dragging you down to its level of immaturity, God brings the best out of you, develops well-formed maturity in you.
>
> Romans 12:1-2 MSG

The New King James Translation of this passage reads this way: "Do not be conformed to this world, but be transformed by renewing your mind..."

On a daily basis, there is so much "junk" that tries to pollute our hearts, such as bitterness, envy, jealousy, fear, lust, and self-pity. That's why we need to continually be transformed by renewing our mind with God's Word. Then we will know the perfect will of God.

The word *renew* means to make new again, to bring back into good condition, to give new spiritual strength to, to restore, refresh, revive, rebuild and rejuvenate. Vines Dictionary defines *renewing your mind* as "the adjustment of the moral and spiritual vision and thinking to the mind of God" [*2]

Have you ever used the Internet, walked away, and then when you came back to the computer, you realized you needed to hit the *refresh* button to update the web page you were on? Why? Because what you saw on your screen may actually have been an outdated page. Since the Internet is constantly reloading, you want to be sure you are viewing up-to-date information.

Every day, God wants to refresh and renew our spirits. To *refresh* means to make clean, revive, give new vigor or spirit to. The word *refresh* implies the supplying of something necessary to restore lost strength, animation, or power. There is a refueling that takes place in the presence of God. Your natural ability can only take you so far, but as you wait on God and spend time in His presence, He will renew your strength and give you fresh insight in the areas that you need it.

In Romans 12, the word *transformed* means to go through a complete change in form or kind. An example of this is *metamorphosis*, the process a caterpillar goes through to change into a butterfly. As you spend time in the Word of God, you will be *transformed* from the inside out. You will begin to do things by the strength of God that you couldn't do before.

We are made up of three parts: spirit, soul and body. Our spirit is what accepted Christ as Savior to become bornagain. Our soul is made up of our mind, will, and emotions. Our body is our physical being, which houses our spirit and soul.

When we received Christ as our Savior, we were born again. Our spirit became a new creation in Christ. *"If anyone is in Christ, he is a new creation; old things have passed away; behold, all things have become new"* (2 Corinthians 5:17 NKJV). Our spirit became new, but our mind still needs to be renewed by the Word of God.

Our attitudes and thought patterns don't change unless they are renewed and transformed by the Word of God. As we spend time reading and meditating on God's Word, it will begin to change the way we live. It will become easier to change our habits because we will have two against one: *our spirit and mind overcoming our body's wrong habits.*

Tug of War: Spirit vs. Flesh

Have you ever been in a battle where your spirit wants to follow after God, but your flesh wants to go in another direction? Your spirit wants to do things for Him and wants to be obedient to whatever He says, but if your flesh has been fed a little bit more than your spirit, the flesh will dominate every time. The flesh will win out because it's a lot stronger.

So many Christians battle with this tug-of-war between the flesh and spirit on the inside of them. Some have struggled with thoughts of fear, lust, perversion, or addiction. Others have struggled with hatred toward someone, and the battle inside them has caused them to hold onto resentment. But if we seek the secret place with God, we will find His strength and power to win that battle.

A friend of my family had previously struggled in the area of pornography. He felt trapped. His marriage and family were falling apart. But he made a decision to repent and began to get help from other men of God. He got accountability and began to renew his mind with the Word. He began to spend time meditating on and confessing the Word of God over and over in his thoughts.

The truth set him free. He was transformed and overcame the battles of his flesh. Besides that, his marriage and family became stronger than ever. This all resulted because he chose to put God's Word first in his life.

Another woman, who is also part of our church, had previously struggled with an eating disorder for years. She said as she spent time in the Word, her mind became renewed to the love God had for her. She also realized the root of her disorder was bitterness she had toward a man who had sexually abused her as a young girl.

When she read the scriptures on forgiveness and God's love, she made a decision to forgive that man. When she did, freedom came in her heart and she no longer struggled with her eating disorder. She was transformed by renewing her mind with the Word of God. Now she and her husband lead missions work all over the world, sharing the liberating power of God with others.

How do you overcome temptations or things that have you bound? First of all, you overcome them by repenting and removing wrong influences and mindsets. Then you must replace those wrong thoughts with what God's Word says about your life. It takes discipline to renew your mind, but it is worth it to experience the freedom that Christ has already paid for. As you feed your spirit the Word of God, it will get stronger and will be able to overcome the temptations of the flesh.

God has given us His truth that sets us free. *"Then said Jesus to those Jews which believed on him, If ye continue in my word (abide in, or stay in my word), then are ye my disciples indeed; And ye shall know the truth, and the truth shall make you free"* (John 8:31-32, explanation mine, KJV). No matter how much we know of the Word, we must continually meditate on it. If we don't continually feed on His Word, we will be going backwards without even realizing it. We will find freedom through God's Word.

Maybe you have not struggled with major addictions but know that God is calling you to step out more in the gifts and callings He has placed on your life. The way to go to the next level in what He is asking you to do is to meditate on the Word of God and gain a greater revelation of who you are in Christ. His Word will empower you to walk out His perfect will for your life.

You can meditate on scriptures like 2 Corinthians 5:21, which says that you are made righteous because of what Jesus has done on the cross. You are no longer a slave to sin (Galatians 2:4). You were once alienated from God, but now because of the blood of Jesus, you are forgiven, accepted, and chosen (Ephesians 1-2). In Christ, you have the wisdom of God and the mind of Christ (1 Corinthians 2:16). You can do all things through Christ who strengthens you (Philippians 4:13). As you meditate on these promises, you will get a revelation of God's love for you, along with the freedom you have in Him.

Get Dressed

When you renew your mind, you get a new set of clothes, so to speak. God takes the filthiness of sin, guilt, shame, fear, and torment and gives you His righteousness, peace, and joy. "Put on your garments of splendor, O Jerusalem, the holy city. The uncircumcised and defiled will not enter you again" (Isaiah 52:1 NIV).

God is saying to His people that they are free from their past. "Putting on your garments of splendor" symbolizes the new garment of righteousness we have been given. When you receive Christ, He cleanses you from your past sins and gives you His righteousness.

Imagine an old, dirty, torn coat being taken off of you, and someone giving you a new, clean one in its place. That is what Christ has done for us on the cross. Second Corinthians 5:21 tells us that in Christ we are made righteous. *Righteous* means right standing with God.

The Bible continues to say that the old things (sin, shame) are passed away and all things have become new. We must wake up and realize that we are no longer a slave to sin, guilt, and shame. We can live alive to righteousness and God's purpose for our lives. "Put off, concerning your former conduct, the old man which grows corrupt according to the deceitful lusts, and be renewed in the spirit of your mind, and that you put on the new man which was created according to God, in true righteousness and holiness" (Ephesians 4:22-24 NKJV). I like the way Romans 13:14 in the Message translation puts it, "Dress yourselves in Christ." How do we dress ourselves in Christ and stay awake to His righteousness? By renewing our mind with what His Word says about us.

A Flourishing Life

Right before Joshua took the Israelites into the Promised Land – the area that they had been striving to get to for forty long years – the Lord stopped him and gave him the secret to having a successful life.

> *"This Book of the Law shall not depart from your mouth, but you shall meditate in it day and night, that you may observe to do according to all that is written in it. For then you will make your way prosperous, and then you will have good success. Have I not commanded you? Be strong and of good courage; do not be afraid, nor be dismayed, for the LORD your God is with you wherever you go."*
>
> Joshua 1:8

Joshua was an incredible man of faith. I admire him because against all odds, he stayed in a spirit of faith. He led the children of

Israel into the Promised Land because he chose to meditate on the Word day and night. He chose to make it a priority in his life.

As you meditate on the Word, you will have fresh strength for every single day. You will have the grace to overcome the temptations and battles that come into your mind, and you will walk in the new things that God has called you to do. In addition, God's Word will cause you to flourish. That word "flourish" means to grow well, to thrive, to be in a place of influence, to be successful, prosperous, generous, and producing good fruit. God has not just called you to survive but to thrive!

> *The righteous shall flourish like a palm tree, He shall grow like a cedar in Lebanon. Those who are planted in the house of the LORD shall flourish in the courts of our God. They shall still bear fruit in old age; They shall be fresh and flourishing, To declare that the LORD is upright; He is my rock, and there is no unrighteousness in Him.*
>
> Psalm 92:12-18 NKJV

The palm tree is mentioned in this passage as an example of how the people of God should be. This tree is known for its beauty, shade, and medicinal properties. It is also known for curing diseases and infections, as well as promoting longevity. It is a source of food, known for its sweetness, shelter and shade. It is recognized as a symbol of grace, elegance, victory, peace, and blessing. The more it's pressed down, the more it grows, which symbolizes its ability to bounce back after hard times. This verse says that even in their old age, the righteous will stay fresh and fruitful.

We can claim this truth for ourselves as followers of Christ, saying "Lord, as we're planted in Your Word, and in the house of the Lord, we're going to stay fresh and flourishing, bearing fruit no matter how many years we're here on this planet."

Psalm 1:1-3 says that those who meditate on the Word of God are like a tree planted by streams of water, bringing forth fruit in its season. As we stay planted in the Word of God, He promises us that we will produce good fruit. What is "good fruit"? Good fruit represents the attributes of God--love, joy, peace, patience, kindness, gentleness, meekness, faith, and self-control. There are times you may feel like nothing is happening on the outside to change your situation, but if you stay planted in the Word you will see the result of fruitfulness and peace.

We cannot produce anything of lasting value in our lives unless we are connected to Jesus and His Word on a daily basis. His Word is the power source. It's like a lamp plugged into an electrical socket. The lamp can have potential, but if it is not plugged in, it cannot produce light. It is the same way in our lives. In order to be God's light in the earth, we must stay plugged in to Him. In John 15, Jesus compares Himself to a vine and us to the branches. As we are connected to His Word and choose to walk in love with one another, we stay fresh and flourishing.

Rivers, Not Reservoirs

God has called us to be rivers of His love, not reservoirs. This principle was illustrated to me when I was in Israel with the picture of the

Sea of Galilee and the Dead Sea. The Sea of Galilee is Israel's largest freshwater lake. It is fed by the Jordan River, which flows through it from north to south. Galilee's shore has rich soil, enabling plants to flourish, and many types of fish live in the Sea of Galilee, providing fishermen with great sustenance.

On the other hand, nothing lives in the Dead Sea. There are no plants or seaweed of any kind around the water. The Dead Sea is continually fed water from rivers and streams coming off the mountains surrounding it, but no rivers drain out of it. As a result, it has become stagnant, and nothing can survive in it.

Likewise, our lives can also become stagnant if we receive a lot of head knowledge from the Bible without giving out of ourselves on a regular basis. God has called us not only to receive from His Word on a daily basis, but also to give out His love and message of hope to others.

7

A LIFE OF LOVE

Be imitators of God as dearly loved children and live a life of love,
just as Christ loved us and gave himself up for us as a fragrant
offering and sacrifice to God." (Ephesians 5:1-2 NIV)

My daughter Elizabeth is 4 years old, and she loves to imitate
me. When I get ready in the morning, she wants to do the
same things I do. She wants to dress like Mommy and do her hair like
Mommy. She also puts on jewelry, makeup, and high heels. She even
wears her purse and scarf like Mommy!

Just as little children imitate their parents, we as children of God
are called to imitate Him in the world we live in. We are called to have
His kind of love that reaches out to the hurting, hopeless, and broken.
Everywhere we go, there are hurting people in need of hope, love, and
encouragement. "So, chosen by God for this new life of love, dress in
the wardrobe God picked out for you: compassion, kindness, humil-
ity, quiet strength, discipline. Be even-tempered, content with second
place, quick to forgive an offense. Forgive as quickly and completely
as the Master forgave you. And regardless of what else you put on,
wear love. It's your basic, all-purpose garment. Never be without it"
(Colossians 3:12-14 MSG).

Love looks awesome on you. It's always in style. God says we are to PUT on love each day, no matter how we feel. It's a choice to love others and even though it's hard sometimes, it's always worth it. "For Christ's love compels us, because we are convinced that one died for all, and therefore all died. And he died for all, that those who live should no longer live for themselves but for Him who died for them and was raised again" (2 Corinthians 5:14 NIV).

Each person is valuable to God. The people you meet in the store, at work, or on the bus are all important to God. Be sensitive and let Him interrupt you so you can share His love with those you come in contact with. It's amazing how quickly joy comes when we get our eyes off ourselves and begin to help someone else. Amy Carmichael, a missionary to India, said, "You can give without loving. But you cannot love without giving."

Not long ago, I was in North Carolina ministering for a weekend. As we were at the airport heading back to Tulsa, we learned that our flight had been canceled and the entire airport had shut down. So, we decided to catch a taxi to an airport in a city close by, in order to catch a flight out the next day.

We were extremely tired and planned to sleep in the car, but as we drove, the cab driver started opening up about her life. Right away, I knew I couldn't sleep. We discovered that she had been through a terrible tragedy in her family. As we encouraged her, God began to move on her heart. We shared with her how much God loved her and how she could have a relationship with Him.

When we got to our destination, I asked if I could pray with her, and she said *yes*. After the prayer, she wept and expressed her gratefulness that we had taken the time to talk to her. When I got out of the cab, I realized that our "delay" was actually a divine opportunity for us to witness to her.

This incident reminded me of the importance of being sensitive and seeing others through the eyes of Jesus. A man in our church, Daryl Burdick, who has now gone on to be with Jesus, used to say, "One moment of your time could mean eternity to someone else." You have the hope that this world needs. You can be a light to others— ONE person at a time!

The People on the Other Side

When God sends us out on a mission, He doesn't stand on the shore while our boat goes out to sea and yell, "I'll be thinking of you! Tell Me how it goes!" No, God goes *with* us!

In Mark 4:35 NKJV, Jesus told his disciples, *"Let us cross over to the other side."* So Jesus and the disciples got into the boat and started to the other side. On the way over, they encountered a great storm, but Jesus was asleep in the boat. "And they [the disciples] awoke Him and said to Him, 'Teacher, do You not care that we are perishing?' Then He arose and rebuked the wind, and said to the sea, 'Peace, be still!' And the wind ceased and there was a great calm." But He said to them, 'Why are you so fearful? How is it that you have no faith?'" (Mark 4:38-40 NKJV).

The disciples forgot that JESUS, the Son of God, was in their boat with them. Never forget that Jesus is in your boat. He will help you make it to the other side. When Jesus and His disciples got to the other side, they met a man who was demon possessed (Mark 5:1-20). When Jesus saw him, He commanded the unclean spirits to come out of him. The man was set free! Afterward, he went and told the entire region of Decapolis all that Jesus had done for him.

Many times, we don't realize there are people on the "other side" of our obedience who need the saving and delivering power of God. We may face storms, but we must remember that Jesus is in the boat with us, and we can make it to the other side and reach the people He has called us to reach.

The Multiplied Effect of Your Obedience

My husband and I were in Quito, Ecuador with a team of youth from our church, ministering throughout the city. One day, we drove up to the public plaza, where we had gotten permission to do street ministry. When we got there, another group was already there. They had a huge stage and sound system set up.

When we got out of the bus, I realized they were performing ancient Incan religious rituals and calling on spirits. They had built altars and were dancing around them, chanting and calling on their "gods" to help them. Hundreds of people had surrounded the group to watch.

When I asked the local youth pastor accompanying us if we could still set up our sound system and minister to the people, he said we had the legal permission to do it. It was up to us whether we still wanted to minister or not. Some of the people we were with were concerned about upsetting the other religious group.

I always try to be very cautious and culturally sensitive when I visit other countries, but at that moment, when I prayed, I knew we didn't need to back down. We needed to proclaim the Gospel to all those present. Then I remembered the story of Elijah and the prophets of Baal from 1 Kings 18. Elijah asked the children of Israel, "How long will you falter between two opinions? If the LORD is God, follow Him; but if Baal, follow him" (vs. 21 NKJV).

The prophets of Baal built an altar to their god, so Elijah built an altar to *his* God and told the people that whichever God answers by fire is the true God (vs. 24). All day, the prophets of Baal yelled, tore their clothes, screamed, and danced—but nothing happened. Then Elijah did something audacious, just to prove how powerful God is. He soaked his altar with water three times. Then he called on God, and fire fell down and consumed the altar. When the people saw this, they fell on their faces before God and said, *"The LORD, He is God!"* (Verse 39 NKJV).

We serve an awesome God! The people at the plaza in Ecuador had been calling on demonic spirits all day to help them, but they were not getting any help. And I knew as we proclaimed the Gospel of Jesus, God would answer by "fire" and show Himself strong in that place. So I told our team to set up our sound system, begin doing the dramas, and start proclaiming that Jesus is the only way, the truth, and the life.

There were a few people from the other religious group who came over and told us to stop, but we kept going. Hundreds of people began to gather around our site to see what we were doing. When we gave our altar call the first time, forty people responded. On the second altar call, sixty more people got saved.

I believe that Jesus not only came to save us from our sins, but from our sickness as well. So next, we asked if anyone needed healing. One woman, who had a terrible pain in her back that restrained her from bending over, came forward. She had just been to the doctor, and he had given her a bag full of medicine. I prayed for her and then told her to bend over. As she acted on her faith, Jesus healed her. When she came back up, she had tears in her eyes and shouted that all the pain was gone.

Her teenage daughter stood there in shock, as she saw her mom healed by the power of God. I asked the woman to share her testimony to encourage others to believe for their healing. When she did, many others raised their hands for prayer and walked away that night with physical miracles.

On top of that, there was a police officer who was watching us while we performed the dramas. He came to me and asked if our team could come and minister to his entire police academy that evening. What favor! When we got there, one hundred officers were waiting for us. At the end of our presentation of the Gospel, every single one of them came forward and gave their lives to Jesus.

One female officer came in late and was standing in the back. I noticed her because she looked so depressed. When I went over to her, the Lord gave me a Word of Knowledge regarding her past. I shared it with her and tears came to her eyes. She was so hopeless that she felt she didn't have any reason to live. Her family had abandoned her at a young age, and since then, she had felt completely alone. I told her how much Jesus loved her. She said she wanted to receive Jesus as her Lord and Savior. After she prayed with me, she looked into my eyes and said, "You came just for me!"

After we finished talking, I realized all that had transpired that day. If we had not ministered in the face of opposition at the plaza that morning, we would not have had the opportunity to go to the police academy or share the Gospel with this precious woman. Our steps of obedience had a multiplied effect on hundreds of people.

Since we chose to push past fear and walk in the power of God's might, we were able to proclaim the Gospel to many hopeless people. You see, there are multitudes in the valley of decision, and we must not be afraid to share with them the hope we have in Jesus.

Live with Eternity in Mind

James 4:14 talks about our life on earth being like a vapor or mist that is visible for a little while, but then disappears. When we live with eternity in mind, we will more readily reach out with the love of God to those who have not heard the Gospel.

When I was 14 years old, our house caught on fire in the middle of the night. That night, my dad's back had been hurting, so he slept in the guest room, where there was a firm mattress. Also, that night I decided to sleep in my mom's room with her, which was rare for me.

At 2 a.m., my dad began to hear beeping sounds. He woke up and discovered the house was filled with smoke. He began to yell and scream, "Wake up! Wake up! Get out of the house! The house is on fire!" As we woke up, we couldn't see well because of all the smoke. Still, my dad, mom, my brother John and I managed to get out of the house.

After we got out and turned around, we realized that my sister Ruthie and my youngest brother Paul were still in the house. My dad's eyes had already been burned from the fire, but he bravely went back in and found Ruthie and pulled her out. Then he went back in for the second time to find my brother Paul, who was only six years old at the time. He was on his hands and knees on the floor in the hallway waiting for someone to come and get him. My dad felt his head, grabbed him by the shirt collar, and pulled him out.

When we all got out and began to run across the street, the front of the house where we had been standing burst into flames. The entire house was consumed, and when the firemen came, they were expecting to pull dead bodies out of the house. They asked whose room was closest to where the fire originated, and I realized it was my room. The firemen proceeded to inform us that due to the location of my room, if I had been in there, I would have been trapped and probably would not have made it out. It was definitely a miracle that we all got out safely.

None of us ever forgot my dad's bravery and love he displayed to us that day. He ended up being hospitalized for a couple weeks after the incident due to damaged eyesight, but he didn't care. He didn't care about his eyes being burned nearly as much as he did about getting all of us out of that burning house. In the hospital he just kept saying, "I got everyone out! I got everyone out! They are all saved!"

This story always reminds me of our responsibility as believers. It's easy to get so concerned with what others think about us or how we appear that we don't take the time to tell them that they are asleep in a "burning house," so to speak. There are people lost and going to hell without the knowledge of Jesus, and we have the opportunity to bring them the truth. I don't say this to bring heaviness to you, but rather an awareness of their eternal destination without Christ.

We must wake up to the urgency of the hour we are living in today. "Keep yourselves in God's love as you wait for the mercy of our Lord Jesus Christ to bring you to eternal life. Be merciful to those who doubt; snatch others from the fire and save them" (Jude 21,23 NIV).

We are called as Christ's ambassadors to fulfill a divine assignment: To share God's message of hope, healing and love with the world in whatever field of work we are in. Hebrews 10:24 tells us that as we see the day of the Lord approaching, we should see how inventive we can be in encouraging love and good works (MSG).

There are opportunities we pass every day to share the love of Jesus. We must listen to His still, small voice and be obedient to the promptings He gives us to reach out to those in need. There have been times that I have missed opportunities and have had to repent for being too busy or selfish to stop. On the other hand, I have also experienced the most amazing times in the presence of God after a moment of loving the "unlovely." When we reach out to those in need, we are actually spending time with Jesus. In these moments, we begin to hear His heartbeat—people.

The Starfish

Several times, I have heard the story of a young boy who was walking along the beach and noticed thousands of starfish washed up on the shore. He knew they would die if they were left out of the water, so he began to pick them up, one by one, and throw them back in the ocean. An older man came by and asked him, "What are you doing?" He replied, "I'm saving the starfish! If I don't throw them in, they will die!"

The old man said, "Son, there are miles of beach and thousands of starfish. What makes you think it really makes a difference?" He listened for a moment, and then picked one up and said, "It makes a difference to this ONE." After that, the old man joined the young boy to help save the starfish.

Sometimes we think that our little part doesn't make a difference, but it does. We can make a difference ONE person at a time. There are opportunities in our church, community, and world to get involved and be a light.

God is calling us to wake up out of depression, fear, and hurt. He's calling us to rise up to the divine assignment He has for us and to walk in His love toward others. There are people all around us who need this, so let's use the freedom Christ has given us to live a life of love.

8
WHAT'S IN YOUR HAND?

On my son Isaac's third birthday, he got his first fishing rod. At first, he didn't know what it was for, so he left it in a corner unopened, while it collected dust. Then, once he opened it, he started using it as a sword to attack his little sister. After that, I thought, *I need to take him fishing to show him what the purpose of this rod really is.*

Since my parents love to fish, they offered to take Isaac and me on a little fishing trip. When we got there, my dad showed Isaac how to bait the hook and throw the line out. Within minutes, he caught a baby fish. He was so excited! It finally dawned on him what the rod was for. Since that day, he has been ready to go fishing every chance he had.

Sometimes, like Isaac, we as believers can forget or not even realize the purpose of the tools God has placed in our hands. He has given each of us gifts, talents, opportunities, influence and resources, but they don't do us any good unless we recognize the purpose for them and the power that's available to us in Christ.

In Exodus 3, we find the story of God calling a man named Moses. He instructed Moses to lead His people out of slavery and into the land to which He had called them. But Moses had a lot of insecurity. In Exodus 4:1, he questioned God, asking, "But suppose they will not believe me or listen to my voice?" (NKJV). God simply replied, "What is in your hand?" Moses answered, "A rod" (NKJV).

Then God said, "Now go; I will help you speak and will teach you what to say, but take this rod in your hand. With it you will do signs and wonders!" (my paraphrase, v. 15-17). The rod in Moses' hand was an ordinary rod. It was used to shepherd sheep. But God wanted him to use that same rod to shepherd the children of Israel out of Egypt. Likewise, God wants to use the ordinary things in our hands--our gifts, talents, resources, ideas, and opportunities--to do extraordinary things for His glory. As we are faithful to use what is in our hand now, God will prepare us for what He has in the future. As Jesus said, those who are faithful with a little He will make ruler over much (Matthew 25:23).

Another biblical example of this is found in the story of David. David was just a shepherd boy tending his father's sheep, day in and day out. Every time a lion or bear came to attack the sheep, he used his slingshot to defeat it. In 1 Samuel 17, when David heard that a huge Philistine giant named Goliath was mocking God and trying to defeat the army of Israel, he stood up to him. He said, "Who is this uncircumcised Philistine that is defying the armies of the living God? I will go and fight him!"

David took what was in his hand—five smooth stones and his slingshot. Then he boldly said to Goliath, "You come against me with a sword and spear and javelin, but I come against you in the name of the LORD Almighty... This day the LORD will hand you over to me... All those gathered here will know that that it is not by sword or spear that the LORD saves; for the battle is the LORD's, and He will give all of you into our hands" (v. 45-47 NIV).

So David took out a stone, slung it, and hit Goliath in the head. To the armies' surprise, the giant fell to the ground. David used what was in his hand to defeat the enemy. And guess what? You can do the same thing. God has put things in your hands to defeat the enemy and bring freedom to others.

One of the women in our church was a stay-at-home mom, raising three children. But she had a desire to make a difference. She had a talent for making jewelry and decided to start her own custom jewelry making business. Every chance she could, she would give a percentage of her profits to missions and to those fighting child trafficking. God began to bless her business tremendously, and today, she has two stores and does business all over the world. She didn't let the excuse of being a stay-at-home mom or living in the USA keep her from making a difference in the world.

Through her generosity, she helped us build a water well in Cambodia and provided clothing, shoes, and books for the orphans in our Hope for Children home. She has also helped us with projects to restore women who have come out of sex trafficking in Asia. She took what was in her hand and let God multiply it to bless others. So not only has she been blessed, but she has also impacted the lives of others on the other side of the world because of her generosity.

In Mark 6:35-39, Jesus was teaching a huge crowd of people. The disciples came to him and said, "Lord these people need to eat." Jesus replied, "You give them something to eat." Then they said, "There is no way we can feed all these people or have the money to buy enough food."

Jesus asked them how many loaves of bread they had. In other words, He was asking, *What do you have in your hand?* They found a little boy with five loaves and two fish. That little boy offered Jesus what he had, and Jesus blessed it and gave it to the disciples to distribute. As they began to hand it out, that little boy's lunch was multiplied and fed over 5,000 people. On top of that, there were twelve baskets left over!

Jesus took what that little boy offered and multiplied it miraculously to bless those people. In the same way, God can take what we offer Him, even though it may seem small and insignificant, and multiply it to bless nations. Start with what you have and watch God work.

Recently, my husband and I were in Thailand holding an evangelistic outreach. I met with the director of Life Impact International. She is a single, Hispanic woman who went to Bible school and moved to Thailand in 2001. She became aware of the rising epidemic of child trafficking and child slavery in Southeast Asia.

She didn't have a lot but started with what she had, and God began to bless her. She helped start rescue homes throughout Thailand, mostly on the Burmese border, and has taken in 93 kids so far. The governor gave her one of his homes to house the kids in to help protect them from traffickers. When they heard about a girl who was about to be sold, they would go and buy the girl from the parents before the traffickers arrived.

Today, these kids are being educated and raised in a loving home because this woman decided not to let her gender keep her from making a difference. She used what was in her hand, and God multiplied it. God can do so much through you if you let Him. You will begin to realize that these gifts were not given to you for your sake only but for the people you will draw to Jesus through your obedience.

The Gift of the Holy Spirit

Besides the unique gifts and talents God has given us, we also share an extremely powerful gift--the gift of His Holy Spirit. "Stir up the gift of God which is in you...for God has not given us a spirit of fear, but of power and of love and of a sound mind" (2 Timothy 1:6-7 NKJV). The Message translation says, "God doesn't want us to be shy with his gifts but bold and loving and sensible."

It is time to stir up the gift of God that is within you. That's what Peter and John did in Acts 3:1-9. Peter and John were on their way to the temple to worship when they met a man who was lame from birth. When he saw Peter and John, he asked them for money. But Peter said, "Silver and gold I do not have but WHAT I DO have I give you: In the name of Jesus Christ of Nazareth, rise up and walk!" (v. 6 NKJV). Taking him by the hand, Peter helped him up, and instantly, the man's feet and ankles became strong. He jumped to his feet and began to walk. Then he left, walking and praising God!

You may feel like you don't have much compared to what someone else has, but I want you to recognize what you *do* have. You have the same Spirit that raised Christ from the dead living inside you. God is not just looking for those who are *able;* He is looking for those who are *available.*

When I was a junior high youth pastor, I took a team of 7th graders to Mexico on a mission trip. I shared with them these same principles. They took hold of them with child-like faith and believed that God could use them. They expected to lay hands on the sick and see them recover.

One day, as we were ministering on the streets, we met a blind woman. She heard us share about Jesus and told the kids, "I believe if you pray for me that I will be healed." That group of 12-year-olds surrounded her and began to pray the prayer of faith. Afterward, they stepped back and the woman began to weep and shout. She could see!

She was so happy and invited us into her home to celebrate what Jesus had done. Were these children able to heal that woman on their own? No! Were they available and open to let God's Spirit work through them? Yes! If God can use a group of 12-year-olds to bring His healing into someone's life, He can use you too.

You have a divine purpose. You are a son or daughter of the Most High God. You have the power of God living on the inside of you. You are creative, and you have unique gifts and talents that God has given you to reach the lost and set the captives free.

You may be a doctor, nurse, businesswoman, stay-at-home mom, baker, designer, artist, teacher, or hairstylist. You may love to work with children or the elderly. You may have a gift of encouragement or discernment. Whatever gifts God has given you, and whatever field you are in, realize that He has put them there for a purpose--to bring freedom to others.

As the Bible says in 1 Corinthians 12 (MSG), just as the human body has many parts, every believer has a part to play in the church and in reaching others. I want to encourage you to start where you are and use what God has put in your hands. Be faithful, and He will make you a ruler over much. When you use what is in your hands, God will do miraculous things.

You Are the Light

Have you ever stumbled around in the dark, and then someone switched on a flashlight and everything suddenly became clear? I believe this is what we are called to do for others with the gifts and talents God has given us. We are called to run into the dark places of the earth and shine the light of Jesus to those who are lost in darkness without Him. "You are the light of the world. A city on a hill cannot be hidden. Neither do people light a lamp and put it under a bowl. Instead they put it on its stand, and it gives light to everyone in the house. In the same way, let your light shine before men, that they may see your good deeds and praise your father in heaven" (Matthew 5:14-16 NIV).

God has put something in your hands that this world needs. If you don't know what it is, I encourage you to find out. How? Ask God to show you. Get involved in your local church. Help out in your community. Start where you are, and soon you will be doing much more than you ever dreamed possible. You are called to be a light!

9

BEING STRETCHED

When I became pregnant with my first child, my stomach began to stretch in order to accommodate the growing baby inside of me. I felt like I expanded more than I wanted to. It's not always comfortable at the time, but you pay the price because you know you are bringing forth new life. You know that your temporary discomfort or pain will be overshadowed by the joy of seeing a new life come into the world.

In the same way, any time you want to grow in an area in your life, you will have to be stretched. *"Enlarge the place of your tent, and let them stretch out the curtains of your dwellings; do not spare; lengthen your cords, and strengthen your stakes. For you shall expand to the right and to the left, and your descendants will inherit the nations, and make the desolate cities inhabited"* (Isaiah 54:2-3 NKJV).

What has God been speaking to you about, that may seem too big or too much? God's vision for your life will cause you to expand. It will cause you to stretch-- give more than you have ever given, love more than you have ever loved, and believe more than you have ever believed. But the fruit of your obedience to God is seeing people's lives transformed for eternity. It's time to expand and enlarge your tent.

When I was pregnant, I also experienced other changes besides my stomach expanding. I changed in the way I slept, ate, and even in the way I walked. Many times, all I could think about was the fact that I was carrying a baby on the inside of me, and it affected most of the decisions I made.

Just like in a physical pregnancy, when God speaks to you about something He has called you to do, you become "pregnant" with that dream or vision. You begin to think about it constantly. Then you begin to take steps to prepare yourself to bring forth that dream or vision. You change the way you do everything. Your daily routine changes because you are thinking about the people who are attached to your purpose. You put aside distractions and unnecessary activities because you know there are lives at stake. In order to enlarge, expand, and reach more people for Christ, we must step out in faith to do what God is asking us to do, regardless of whether it requires us to do something new or go somewhere unfamiliar.

It's a New Season

Not long ago, I took my kids, Isaac and Lizzy, to the zoo. The first thing they wanted to ride was the carousel because it was at the entrance. It seemed fun at first, but after going around a couple times, I thought, *Why are we going around on this carousel when there are so many REAL animals in the zoo to explore? We are not GOING anywhere!*

As soon as I had that thought, Isaac said, "Mom, I'm ready to go ride some REAL animals!" When we got off, we discovered there were

REAL camels they could ride. So we all rode the camels and had so much fun discovering all the unique animals in the zoo.

Later, I found myself relating that experience to my spiritual walk. I realized how easy it is to just settle for riding the "carousel" of routine and comfort, doing things the way things have always been done. This is a place of fear, but God wants to take us to a place of faith. There is new territory He has called us to take for the kingdom.

Moses had a similar revelation in Deuteronomy 1. Verses 6-8 say, *"The Lord our God said to us at Horeb, 'You have stayed long enough at this mountain… Go in and take possession of the land…"* The children of Israel originally only had an 11-day journey to the Promised Land, but instead it took them 40 years to arrive.

Finally Moses said, "Enough! It's time to go possess the land God has provided for us." That's exactly what I felt God speak to me through this simple carousel ride at the zoo that day. He said, *You've been at this place long enough. It is time to go possess the land that I have given you!*

Let's not get comfortable in the things God has done for us in the past. Let's believe Him for more. God wants to do exceedingly and abundantly above all we ask or think according to the power that is at work in us.

Launch Out into the Deep!

In Luke 5, Jesus borrowed Peter's fishing boat to teach the people. Afterward, He came to Peter and said, "Launch out into the deep and let down your nets for a catch" (v.4 NKJV). Peter answered, "Master, we've worked hard all night and haven't caught anything. but because you say so, I will let down the nets" (v.5 NIV).

Think about this for a minute. Peter was a professional fisherman-- he knew everything in the natural necessary to catch fish. But when Jesus spoke to him to do something audacious, costly, and even risky, he did it. He trusted, obeyed, and launched out into the deep.

There are times in our lives that Jesus will ask us to do something that doesn't make sense in the natural. He may ask us to give a certain amount, go somewhere we have never gone, or reach out in new ways that are uncomfortable for us. In those times, we must trust that our faith and obedience will make way for the miraculous.

The story goes on to say, "When they had done this, they caught a great number of fish, and their net was breaking. So they signaled their partners in the other boats to come and help them. And they came and filled both boats so full that they began to sink" (v.6-7 NKJV).

Notice that Peter had to signal to other partners to come help them bring in the harvest. I believe it's the same way in the Body of Christ. We must work together to bring in the full harvest. There is such a great harvest coming that we will not be able to handle it on our own. So get ready. You may feel frustrated because you have "fished all night" or done all you know to do in the natural, but remember at the Word of God, everything can change.

Just like He did to Peter, I believe God is speaking to people today to launch out into the deep and get off that carousel ride. As William

Carey said, "Expect great things from God; attempt great things for God." As I shared earlier, when God told us to launch out to the mission field, it was a huge step of faith. We had to choose to trust and obey God even though we didn't see the full picture of everything He had in store for us.

I have discovered that God doesn't just tell us to launch out in one way, but He will continue to ask us to launch out in other ways as well. If we are willing and available to Him, He will call us to stretch in new ways on a regular basis, in order for us to grow and reach more people through our lives.

He might call you to start a new business venture, move to a new location, or give sacrificially. The exciting thing is that whatever God asks of you, He will give you the strength to expand. That's what happened to Abraham. God told him, "Get out of your country, from your family and from your father's house, to a land that I will show you...I will bless you...And in you all the families of the earth shall be blessed" (Genesis 12:1-3 NKJV).

Abraham left his home and went to the place God told him. In that place, God blessed him. In the same way, as you are obedient to trust and obey God, you will see His blessing and a harvest of souls brought into the kingdom. The new thing God wants you to do may not be to move to another city or country like Abraham or like my family, but it still requires faith. Whether it's moving into greater intimacy with God, obedience to something He has asked you to do, freedom in an area of your life, or a place of serving in a greater way for God's kingdom, the key is to be willing and open to God and focus on His call.

Not long ago, the Lord spoke to me about hosting our SHINE women's conferences in new nations. The goal of these gatherings is to encourage women in their value and identity in Christ, as well as encourage them in the important part they play in the body of Christ. It is an opportunity for churches in these regions to unite. We had hosted some of these conferences in the USA, but I knew God was speaking to me to launch out to reach more women. That meant there were new things we needed to believe God for to cover the cost of these conferences. As we began to pray and ask God for this, He began to open doors in these nations and connect us with the people and churches to work with. By God's grace, we were able to host these women's conferences this past year in Nepal, Hong Kong, Cambodia, Thailand, and Russia.

It has been miraculous to see the thousands of women who have been transformed and healed because of the truth of God's Word that is preached. When we choose to give sacrificially and believe Him for provision, He does a supernatural work!

Maybe you're afraid to step out into the dreams and visions God has put in your heart. Maybe you're waiting for all the resources to be there. If so, you need to understand that many times they don't come until we start taking steps of faith and obedience. Then miracles happen and God gets all the glory. God may speak to you to sow a big seed into someone else's ministry, and you could be thinking, "I really need it myself!" But as you sow what God speaks, He will meet your needs.

I am reminded of the time that my dad had first started Victory Christian Center. They were in a building that was too small for their growing congregation but they were struggling just to pay the rent. He was praying they would not only have enough money to pay the rent but also to move into a larger facility.

The church owned a large tent and God spoke to my dad to give the tent to a missionary. He thought, *I could sell it and have some money for a new building.* But he knew even if he did that, it would not be enough to pay the bills. He realized it would be better if he gave that tent and sowed it as a seed. So he did and shortly after that, God blessed the church with all the money needed to not only pay their bills, but God opened the door for them to begin meeting in one of the largest convention centers in our city. God did exceedingly, abundantly, above all! When we trust God as our source and give what He says to give, He is more than able to multiply what we give to Him.

God wants to do great things in and through you. Believe that He is able to do the impossible in your life—that he is able to bring a road in the wilderness *(direction)*—and streams in the desert *(provision)*.

See with Eyes of Faith

In Joshua 6, Joshua and the children of Israel were getting ready to enter Jericho. They had just crossed the Jordan River, which was a miracle in itself, and now they were facing the city's great wall. In

Joshua 6:2, God told Joshua beforehand, *"See! I have given Jericho into your hand" (NKJV).*

God began to give Joshua instructions on exactly how to do it. He wanted Joshua to see it on the *inside*, before he saw it on the *outside*. Do you see your dreams clearly on the inside? Where is your focus? Are you looking at your problems or how great God is?

We must see our dreams on the inside, before we see them on the outside. We need to keep the vision before us, and see with eyes of faith the things God has prepared for us to walk in and the promises He has given us to possess. God wants to show us things in the spirit that we are called to do and walk in.

So how do we see with eyes of faith? We must fix our eyes on God's Word and meditate on His promises and faithfulness. We must tune out the distractions of the world and focus our heart to hear and see what He is saying. We will always move toward what we focus on.

During the holidays, we planned to take a vacation and told our kids we were going to the beach. We still had a few weeks before leaving, but right away our kids ran, put on their swimsuits, got their towels, and started laying out in the living room. They had already begun to make *preparations*. They were already *imagining* themselves at the beach. That's the kind of child-like faith we need--faith that sees what God has in store for us and causes us to prepare ourselves for it. If God has spoken something to you, begin to see yourself walking in that promise by faith and start making preparations for it to come to pass. Ask God to help you see with eyes of faith and let Him show you His strategy for what He wants you to do.

Get God's Strategy

God has unique strategies for you to help fulfill His purpose for your life. He has ways of doing things that haven't been done before. God has a particular way He wants to use you to reach people for His Kingdom.

In Joshua 6:3, God told the children of Israel to march around the wall for seven days, and on the seventh day to march around seven times and then blow their trumpets and shout. They had never done this before. This might have seemed crazy to some people, but Joshua listened and obeyed what God said. He began to speak to his army and tell them this was how they were going to take over Jericho. He spoke; then they walked it out.

God's Word says if you need wisdom, you can ask Him and He will give it to you (James 1:5). So if you are wondering what the next step is, just ask God. Seek Him for His divine purpose for your life and how it relates to helping others. Once God gives you that direction or strategy, write it down. Then begin to take the steps necessary to carry it out.

Write Down the Vision

Write down the vision that God put in your heart. Think of visions He has given you from previous days, months, or years. Write down the things He speaks to you, because they will come to pass. Believe them and release your faith. Remember, you are not being selfish because the dream God has put in you is not just about you. It's about the people you are going to touch and reach. Hang on to it.

Post it on your wall. Declare it. Release your faith for those dreams and visions to come to pass.

Habakkuk 2:2 NKJV says, *"Write the vision and make it plain."* After you write it down, start taking steps. Start trusting God. Start doing what He says to do and it will surely come. It won't come in your own might, but by the grace and power of His Holy Spirit you can walk out the divine assignment He has called you to walk in.

Run with the Vision!

Our life is compared to a race in Hebrews 12, "Since we are surrounded by such a great cloud of witnesses, let us throw off everything that hinders and the sin that so easily entangles, and let us run with perseverance the race marked out for us. Let us fix our eyes on Jesus, the author and perfector of our faith, who for the joy set before him endured the cross, scorning its shame, and sat down at the right hand of the throne of God" *(v.1-2 NIV)*. In order to run the race that God has set before us and be a light, we must fix our eyes on Jesus and lay down anything that would hinder us.

There are many distractions that try to come against us on a daily basis, pulling us away from that call. But just like a runner strips off anything that would slow him down, we must also do so on a regular basis. We must let go of bitterness, fear, selfishness, pride, anger, lust, discouragement, and any sin that would hinder us.

We should press toward the mark of the high call of God in Christ Jesus. We cannot be those who just "maintain" what God has already provided, we must move forward and possess the new things God has set before us. This is not a time to hesitate; it's a time to run. He is the author and finisher of our faith. He is cheering us on in this race. He is for us. He is with us, so run!

Shout!

Another important thing to notice about the battle of Jericho, besides the fact that the Israelites won it, is how they won it. They won it through praise. Joshua 6:16 says when they obeyed and shouted to God with the voice of victory, the walls came down.

What walls or obstacles are you up against? Are you believing for healing, direction, or a dream to be fulfilled? Find out what God's Word says about your situation, then speak it and act on what He says to do. When we do what we can do, God can do what only He can do in us and for us, for His glory.

God has given you a divine assignment to complete for the kingdom. But you won't accomplish it if you don't first see it on the inside, begin to call it forth, and then begin to act on what He has said.

Step Out

This is not the time to draw back into a cave and hide. This is the time to step out into the new things that God has called you to do. Maybe you have allowed fear or comparison to hold you back from using your gifts and talents for God. You might have compared yourself like Gideon and said, "God, I'm the weakest. I'm the least. Why me?" But God says, "Because I've called you. I've appointed you."

Jesus gave all of us the Great Commission before He ascended into heaven when He said, "Go into all the world and preach the good news to all creation" (Mark 16:15 NIV). Romans 10:14-15 NIV says, "How, then, can they call on the one they have not believed in? And how can they believe in the one of whom they have not heard? ...How beautiful are the feet of those who bring good news!"

We are Christ's ambassadors in the earth today. We are called to bring the good news of salvation to those who are lost in darkness (2 Corinthians 5:20). The Bible also says that we give off a sweet scent (aroma) of Christ to those who are on the way to salvation (2 Corinthians 2:15 MSG). He has called us to be His hands and feet in the earth. Our purpose is wrapped up in bringing others closer to Jesus.

I believe God will show you people that you are supposed to witness to. It could be a co-worker or friend who you have been afraid to talk to. God is saying, *Don't be afraid. Step out and begin to speak.* You may say, "But I don't even know what I would say." Well, just like God said to Moses and Gideon, He says to you, *I will give you the words to say.* When God puts someone on your heart to minister to, He will give you the words to say. You don't have to be afraid to be a witness and a light to your friends, family members, and coworkers.

Every believer, regardless of his or her vocation, is called to be a witness for Christ. When you begin to do the works of God and disciple others by pouring into them and being a light to them, you step into the purpose God has designed you for. You begin to grow spiritually and life becomes so exciting. Serving God can be amazing every single day.

God may be calling you to step out into new areas of leadership within your church by serving, giving of yourself, or starting a Bible study or cell group. Don't stay in your comfort zone, in your cozy little cave, or on your cozy little couch. If you don't step out, you won't grow. This is where so many Christians are. They think they know so much because they have continually sat under the church's teaching, yet they haven't done anything with the knowledge they have gained.

Maybe you already know the ideas and dreams that God has put in your heart, but you still need wisdom concerning the strategy. God wants to direct you in how to walk it out. He will give you wisdom and insight as you ask Him. But He won't tell you the next step until you obey the first one.

Maybe you have had great opposition and attacks from the enemy over what God has called you to do. Paul said there was a great door of opportunity for him, but he also knew he had many adversaries (1 Corinthians 16:9). Your friends and family may be well meaning when they discourage you from stepping out and obeying God. Others may laugh or make fun of you for being so bold, but don't be discouraged.

If you are facing obstacles in your mind, cast down those imaginations of fear and comparison and put your trust in the Lord. Believe that God is for you and that no weapon formed against you will prosper (Isaiah 54:17). Don't hide your light.

This is your moment to rise up out of fear and complacency. It is time to get out of the cave and use the gifts God has placed in your hand for His name to be known in the earth. You are called for such a

time as this. Make a decision today to arise and step out in the things
God has spoken to you.

10

TRAVEL LIGHT

God wants to do a new thing in your life, but you must make room for Him to move. Life can get so full of distractions and sin that it weighs you down and stops you from receiving the new things He is trying to give you. "Do not remember the former things, nor consider the things of old. Behold, I will do a new thing, now it shall spring forth; ...I will even make a road in the wilderness and rivers in the desert" (Isaiah 43:18-19 NKJV).

When we were in the process of selling our home and packing up to move to the mission field, I realized we had accumulated a lot of unnecessary stuff (junk). Our garage was full of stuff we had to sort through and get rid of. In fact, when we finally left to go on the mission field, we only brought eight suitcases for all four of us (not including two car seats). I realized there were a lot of things that were unnecessary for us to take to our new place. It was more expensive and more trouble for us to take most of the old things we had, than to just get new things when we got there.

Spiritually speaking, it's the same way. Many times we try to hang on to the old things—old habits and old mindsets—but those things will only slow us down when we go where God wants to take us. He wants us to lay those things down so there will be room for Him to do a *new thing* in our lives, and use us to help others. "Brothers, I do not consider myself yet to have taken hold of it. But one thing I do: Forgetting what is behind and straining toward what is ahead, I press on toward the goal to win the prize for which God has called me heavenward in Christ Jesus" (Philippians 3:13-14 NIV).

None of us have arrived. None of us is perfect. But we can still follow Paul's example and forget the things that are behind: Our past failures, offenses, and other things that have held us back. We can reach forward to the new things that God has for us and to the call He has on our lives.

One summer, we went on a month-long ministry trip and I strategically packed our bags so we would travel light. I packed clothes and of course, my kids' favorite toys, Buzz Lightyear and princess dolls. As the month drew to a close, I started packing for our trip back home and realized we had collected a lot of stuff during our stay.

Our kids had collected rocks and random items from their outdoor adventures, along with a huge homemade cardboard racetrack they made to run their cars on. So, we had to sit down and sort through what was really important to them and what we could leave behind.

We must do the same thing in our daily lives as we travel on our journey with God. We must let go of things that weigh us down and keep us from moving forward. Paul said in Philippians 3:13 NIV, "ONE THING I do: Forgetting what is behind and straining toward what is ahead, I press on toward the goal to win the prize for which God has called me heavenward in Christ Jesus." The Message translations says, "Friends, don't get me wrong: By no means do I count myself an expert in all of this, but I've got my eye on the goal, where God is beckoning us onward- to JESUS. I'm off and running, and I'm not turning back."

Our goal is to know Jesus and fulfill His purpose for our lives. But in order to run free, we have to let go of hurt, bitterness, jealousy, judgment toward others, disappointment, comparison, guilt, shame, complacency, and weariness. Many times we don't even know the load we are carrying unless we take time to sit before God, read His Word, and listen to what He is saying.

Recently, I went to the chiropractor to get my neck and back adjusted after traveling. I couldn't figure out why I was in so much pain. The chiropractor asked me what I had been carrying and I answered, "Children, suitcases, laundry, etc." Then he asked me what was in my purse. I thought, *Now he is really getting personal.*

You have to understand that I have a "mother" purse, like the mom in the movie, *One Fine Day.* I carry everything I might need for an emergency. When I looked inside my purse, I found a couple of water bottles, toys, books, vitamins, snacks, and all kinds of things that were *weighing* my purse down. I realized I needed to take time to get rid of unnecessary things in my purse, so I wouldn't be in so much pain from all the extra weight.

Just like when I went to the chiropractor, when we spend time in God's presence and His Word, He begins to reveal to us things we need to let go of. Sometimes those things are considered "good," but they are distracting our focus from what God is saying to us.

For instance, there are things we are called to carry in one season, but not in another. As we seek God's wisdom, He will guide us in our relationships, work, marriage, family, and ministry. He will also help us prioritize what He wants us to focus on in each season. He will restore our soul as we put our faith in Him. In His presence, we can lay our burdens down. "Are you tired? Worn out? Burned out on religion? Come to me. Get away with me and you'll recover your life. I'll show you how to take a real rest. Walk with me and work with me watch how I do it. Learn the unforced rhythms of grace. I won't lay anything heavy or ill-fitting on you. Keep company with me and you'll learn to live freely and lightly" (Matthew 11:28-30 MSG).

The Word is like a mirror; it reads our heart. As we spend time in God's Word, the Lord will speak to us about specific areas of our lives and then He will give us the grace to overcome in those areas. Hebrews 4:12 tells us that the Word divides between the soul and the spirit and judges the thoughts and intents of the heart.

"What Are You Packing?"

Fear or Faith?

Bitterness or Forgiveness?

Worry or Worship?

Disappointment or Hope?

Judgment or Love?

Weariness or God's Strength?

Guilt or Grace?

The enemy wants to choke the Word and keep it from growing and producing fruit in our heart. Mark 4:18 talks about the Word being like seed in our hearts. But if we allow the worries of this life and the desire for things to overwhelm us, then those things will choke the Word from bearing fruit in our heart and lives.

Hear What God Is Saying

God is speaking vision to His Church and to us individually, but we must remain tuned in and ready to hear with ears of faith. With all the voices vying for our attention, we must be still and hear what He is saying. His words unlock mysteries.

When the children of Israel were headed toward the Promised Land, God told them: "Today if you hear his voice, do not harden your heart as you did in the rebellion, during the time of testing in the desert, where your fathers tested and tried me and for fourty years saw what I did…see to it, brothers, that none of you have a sinful, unbelieving heart that turns away from the living God…. Today, if you hear His voice, do not harden your hearts …" (Hebrews 3:7-9, 12, 15 NIV). We must be those who hear with faith and keep our hearts softened to His leading.

Revelation Knowledge

"The secret of the LORD is with those who fear Him, and He will show them His covenant" (Psalm 25:14 NKJV). God wants to reveal secrets to us but He will only reveal them to those who fear Him. In its original translation, the word *fear* doesn't imply that we are afraid of God; it means we reverentially honor, obey, and pursue Him. It doesn't mean that we are perfect, but that we have a sense of awe towards God. The fear of God is to hate evil and to pursue what is good. So if we fear Him and seek after Him, God said He will direct and guide us. One illustration of this is found in the book of Daniel 2. In this story, King Nebuchadnezzar had a terrible dream and knew it meant something about his future. He sought all the wise people in the land to interpret this dream, but he couldn't find anyone who could. Finally he heard about Daniel, who was known for seeking the Lord.

Daniel prayed three times a day, fasted, and sought God with all of his heart. So the king called him in. When Daniel heard the king's dream, he began to pray that God would reveal its meaning to him. And He did. Through Daniel's interpretation of the dream, God revealed what King Nebuchadnezzar's future was going to look like (Daniel 2:19-23).

God can give us spiritual understanding in things that other people don't understand in the natural. He wants to give us revelation knowledge. You may or may not see a vision or a dream, but God does promise to guide you and to reveal to you things to come as you seek Him.

If God has put a dream or vision in your heart, trust His timing to bring it to pass. "Though it [the dream or vision] tarries, wait for it; because it will surely come..." (Habakkuk 2:3 NKJV). Maybe you have seen a little bit of the vision come to pass and said, *God, is this it? Is this all I'm going to see?* I want to encourage you to hold on to the vision. Continue to press hard after God. Stay in the secret place of His wisdom and seek Him. Be obedient to take the steps that He tells you to take now, and He will open doors to other opportunities in the future.

Take the Limits Off

When I went to Thailand to speak at a women's conference, I stayed at the mission base of a fellow missionary and friend. Since I enjoy running in the mornings, they told me that I could go outside the compound in the morning to run around the block. I was excited because Thailand is a beautiful country with mountains all around and many sites to explore.

The next morning, I woke up and got ready to take a jog. But when I went to the gate, it was locked. I went to the other side, but it was also locked. I was fenced in, but I was ready to run. It was early and I didn't want to wake anyone up, so I just sat there at the gate. The Lord began to speak to me and He showed me there are many times that there are things He has called us to do, but we have "self-imposed" gates that are locked.

The Bible says we were created for good works that we should walk in, but sometimes we are "fenced in" or held back because of fear, discouragement, apathy, or selfishness. God reminded me of the passage in 2 Corinthians 6:11-13 (MSG), "…I long for you to enter the wide open spacious life…we didn't fence you in…live openly and expansively."

The Lord began to speak to me about the importance of taking the "limits off" my faith and believing He can do greater things through believers to reach more people with His love and bring Him glory in the earth. I encourage you to do the same. He is able to do above and beyond what we could imagine. Nothing is impossible with Him.

It's easy to get comfortable in things God has already done, feeling like we have enough, "for us four and no more." But we must continue to believe for more. Our faith is not just for ourselves; it's for the people we are called to reach. When God moves in our lives, people are influenced and God is glorified.

I believe there are two keys that open the door to the miraculous in our lives: Faith and love. The Bible says, "Without faith it is impossible to please God" (Hebrews 11:6 NIV). Faith works by love; you cannot have one without the other. Faith and love are the keys that open up things in the spirit realm—love for God and love for people (1 John 3:23).

Galatians 5:1,6,13-14 NIV says, "It is for freedom that Christ has set us free. Stand firm, and then, do not let yourselves be burdened again by a yoke of slavery... the only thing that counts is faith expressing itself through love...You, my brothers, were called to be free. But do not use your freedom to indulge the sinful nature, rather, serve one another in love. The entire law is summed up in a single command: 'Love your neighbor as yourself.'"

In 2010, Caleb and I were ministering in Sri Lanka. We were inspired hearing the testimony of the pastor we were working with, Dr. Colton Wicknamratne, who had such a vision to reach his city. Even though the nation was predominately Buddhist, God spoke to him to build a large church that seated 5,000 people. An auditorium that size had never been built there before, and he was told it was impossible because of the poverty and persecution of the Buddhist community. He went through persecution and was put in jail at times but he unashamedly walked in faith and obedience, and supernaturally all the funds came in. Now they have four services every Sunday, reaching thousands of people. Dr. Colton took the limits off with his faith in God and his love for people.

Sometimes we limit what God can do through us, not only those called into full-time ministry, but every believer in every sector of society. God has you where you are to be a light in the world, to exalt Him with your gifts, talents, and resources for the glory of God.

For the sake of the people on the other side, you must live a life of faith and love. There are people who need what you have. Don't hold back. When we are motivated by love and operate in faith, miracles happen. You may be called to step out in new things, but it might be uncomfortable. You may feel like you don't know how to do it, but as you take one step at a time, God will give you the next one.

People Who Arose to Their Destiny

One person in the Bible who had to "do it afraid" was Jeremiah. When God called Jeremiah, He said, ""Before I formed you in the womb I knew you; Before you were born I sanctified you; I ordained you a prophet to the nations." Then said I, 'Ah Lord God! Behold, I cannot speak, for I am a youth. But the Lord said to me: 'Do not say "I am a youth," for you shall go to all to whom I send you, and whatever I command you, you shall speak. Do not be afraid of their faces, for I am with you to deliver you,' says the Lord" (Jeremiah 1:5-8 NKJV).

Jeremiah was just a young man when God called him to be a voice for his generation. God uses ordinary people to do extraordinary things in this world. You have been called to do mighty works for God, but the first thing you must do is step out of the cave of fear. God sees beyond who you are right now--He sees you as who He has assigned you to be.

Mary, the mother of Jesus, also had to push past fear. When the angel told her that she would conceive the Son of God supernaturally, I'm sure she was scared. She had to trust God completely, even though it possibly meant she would be shunned from everyone including her family and future husband (Luke 1:30-45 NLT). Like Mary, we must believe that with God all things are possible and that He will fulfill the things He has spoken to us. We must be like Mary and say, *I am your servant, Lord. May Your will be done in my life.*

11

JOY ON THE JOURNEY

Late one night, I was driving with my kids to pick up Caleb from the airport. When I decided to take a new route, my very inquisitive son began to ask me about twenty questions like, "Mom, where are we going? Mom, are you sure this is the right way? It doesn't look like it." I had to reassure him that I knew what I was doing, so I said, "It's okay, Isaac. We are going on a new road but we will get there. Mommy knows where she is going."

Later, he started asking more questions like: "Mom, is Daddy going to be there? Is he going to bring me a toy? How long does it take to get there? Why is it taking so long?" And then came the infamous question, "Mom, are we there yet?" (How many parents have heard that one?) I calmed him by saying, "Isaac, it's okay, Daddy will be there and we will be there just in time. Be patient, trust me, and enjoy the ride."

After that conversation, I thought about how we can be the same way with God when He is directing us into a new season of growth or new territory for His kingdom. We start asking God questions like my son Isaac did: "When? How? Where? Who? "Anyone who intends to come with me has to let me lead. You're not in the driver's seat; I am" (Matthew 16:24 MSG). The New International Version says it like this: "If anyone would come after me, he must deny himself and take up his cross and follow me."

God reminds us, "Trust in Me with all your heart, lean not to your own understanding, in all your ways acknowledge Me and I will direct your steps" (Proverbs 3:5-6). God wants us to trust and obey His voice while enjoying the journey. I like how Joyce Meyer puts it, "You may not be where you want to be but you are not where you used to be. Learn to enjoy where you are on the way to where you are going!"

Trust God's Timing

One of the biggest areas I had to learn to trust God in was in believing for the right husband. When I went to college, I was so excited to meet new people. I was at a Christian university and thought for sure I would meet my husband there. During the first few weeks, the Lord spoke to my heart not to date the first year. I thought, *WHAT?! God I've been waiting so long already. I thought I was going to find my man of God.* I was worried that I would miss the right guy for me, or he would miss me if I wasn't available.

During my first semester, I was asked to be a chaplain in my dorm and my dad also asked me to be one of the children's pastors in a new service they were starting at our church. In addition to that, I had a part-time job in the Alumni Office on campus and worked part-time at a local store. I knew the Lord wanted me to focus on what He had put in my hands, instead of looking for a guy.

It wasn't easy, though, because soon, a guy at my school started pursuing me. I began to think, *He is popular. He is such a great guy.*

Everyone says I should date him. I was flattered and thought if I didn't date him, I would lose him to some other girl. I became impatient and started dating him.

I dated him for two years, and we even started serving at the church together. When he asked me to marry him, I didn't have complete peace but thought it was just wedding jitters, so I said *yes.*

Ten days before the wedding, things really came to a head and both of us realized we did not have peace about getting married at that time. It was a hard decision to make, but I decided to call it off completely. Afterwards, I asked God what I did wrong in the process, and He brought me back to the beginning—I didn't obey His voice when He said to wait.

The Lord began to deal with me about not trusting Him with that area of my heart. I was impatient and rushing ahead because I was afraid I would miss out. So, I am speaking from experience when I encourage you to trust God with your relationships. Don't rush it or compromise. One of the verses I have clung to is in Matthew 6:33-34 in the Message. It says, "Don't worry about missing out. You'll find all your everyday human concerns will be met. Give your entire attention to what God is doing right now, and don't get worked up about what may or may not happen tomorrow. God will help you deal with whatever hard things come up when the time comes." Keep God's Word first in your life. It is your compass.

After waiting a year and a half after that breakup, my future husband, Caleb, began to pursue me. We had been friends since high school and during that time, we had gone on a mission trip to Africa.

On that trip, Caleb surrendered his life to Jesus and to the call of God to work in the ministry. He told me that during that trip he knew he wanted to marry me, but he didn't say anything because he realized he wasn't ready. He made a decision to prepare himself and seek God's purpose for His life.

Six years after that trip, we went on our first date, and he shared his heart and the vision he had for his life with me. It was like I met him for the first time. It was as if he was reading my heart to me. He had been volunteering at church all those years, getting trained and focusing on God. He became a new man.

Our heart and passion for the Lord were in sync. Our focus on the call God had for us to the nations matched. I realized he was everything I had prayed for, and there was an overwhelming peace that we were both at a place in which we were ready for marriage. I discovered firsthand the truth in Ecclesiastes 3:11, God makes all things beautiful in His time.

Joy Is in Believing

I want to encourage you to trust God completely because He is the Creator of the Universe. He's the Creator of your life. He has good plans for you. You can trust Him with your life. You don't have to be in constant fear about where you are headed. You can have joy during the journey. Romans 15:13 says joy and peace are found in believing. Tom Newberry said in his book, *The 4:8 Principle*, "Joy is an outward sign of inward faith in the promises of God."

We should walk in joy every day of our lives. This kind of joy is not based on hype; it's based on our hope in Jesus Christ. It's a joy that is rooted and grounded in our faith in Jesus Christ—that no matter what happens, no matter what circumstances come our way, our hope is founded and anchored in Jesus Christ. That is the kind of joy that nothing, or no one, can take away. In John 15:11, it says that in Jesus there's fullness of joy. By abiding in Him and following Him in the love walk that He has called us to walk in, there's fullness of joy.

Rejoice

Paul wrote in Philippians 4:4, NIV "Rejoice in the Lord always. I will say it again: Rejoice!" It's interesting that he wrote the book of Philippians while he was in prison--one of the worst circumstances someone could possibly be in. Yet throughout this book, he tells the Philippians to rejoice. This doesn't make sense in the natural.

Why would he be saying, *Rejoice?* Because Paul understood that he needed to make the most of every opportunity. He didn't let his circumstances keep him from making a difference or from sharing the love and joy of the Lord. Even in prison, he was making the most of every opportunity as he wrote to the Philippian church.

You may be facing trouble in your marriage, family, finances, or job. Maybe you are facing huge problems or worrying about every-thing that's ahead. I want to encourage you to lift up your eyes and worship God. We can rejoice in every season and every circumstance.

Acts 16 talks about how Paul was in prison, and at midnight he and Silas began to worship and praise God. As they did this, an earthquake began to shake the prison. The doors flew open and their chains fell off. Paul and Silas walked out of prison completely free.

When the jailer saw what was happening, he was afraid and tried to kill himself. But Paul and Silas were full of the Spirit and said, "No, no, no, no. We're all here." The jailer knelt down and said, "What must I do to be saved?" Right then and there, the jailer gave his heart to Jesus Christ. Later that night, his whole family got saved. This happened because of the testimony of Paul and Silas—they chose to rejoice, even in prison. What a testimony for us in our everyday lives.

Caleb and I have spent time in nations in which pastors and believers are persecuted and beaten for their faith. Yet, their joy is astounding. Recently, we spent time with an older pastor who had been persecuted for boldly preaching the Gospel in a nation that was violent and resistant to the Gospel. Even in the midst of a nation that had political unrest, poverty, and persecution, we heard testimonies of thousands of people who had been touched and affected because of his witness for Christ.

We were so humbled to be in his presence. There was such a glow about him. He had the joy of the Lord. He had peace beyond human understanding. I thought, *If he can rejoice, what do we have to complain about?* What an example he was to us. His witness gave us a greater perspective and encouraged us to rejoice no matter what.

You may be facing terrible things. You may be facing hardship, trouble or worries, but there's power when you praise God. There's power when you choose to rejoice, even when it hurts, even when it doesn't feel good, and even when you don't want to. That's real joy. Joy is not based on our circumstances; it's based on our hope and faith in Jesus Christ.

Why is it so important for us to rejoice? "The joy of the LORD is your strength" (Nehemiah 8:10 NIV). The devil wants to steal our joy because he wants to steal our strength. If he can steal our strength, he will keep us from fulfilling our divine assignment. We need strength to walk out the purpose and plans of God. But if we lose our joy and our sense of strength and purpose, we won't step out and obey what God is saying. Don't let the enemy steal your joy. Your joy is your strength.

It is important to remember this truth during our mountaintop experiences, as well as in our valley times. Remember this when your car breaks down. Remember this when you have a flat tire. Remember this when something bad happens in a friendship or a relationship at work. In every situation, the Bible commands us to rejoice. It's a mark of believers.

One time, while living in Hong Kong, I really had to remind myself of this truth. Caleb was headed to Mongolia with some other pastors to minister at a pastors' conference. I wasn't really looking forward to him going on that trip, because we were just getting settled in Hong Kong, and I was still getting used to all the changes of living in a different country. He would be in a place where he wasn't sure when he would be able to call or email us.

I had not ventured to drive on the other side of the road yet and remember thinking, *Oh, God, this is going to be a little challenge for me. I'm going to need to learn how to get around on the Metro train with a stroller and two toddlers.* I remember praying, *Lord, I need joy. I need strength in this season because I know this is a divine opportunity for Caleb to preach to pastors who are hungry for the Word. I ask that as I send him, You would give the kids and me supernatural joy this week, in Jesus' name.*

At that time, I was working with a local church in Hong Kong and was scheduled to lead worship that week. It took a while to get to the church from where we were, so I thought, *Okay, I need to get up a couple hours earlier than normal so I can catch the public transport and get there on time.* As I was strategically planning our stops for that morning, I realized that my kids had made a complete mess. I quickly cleaned them up and headed out the door to go to church.

As we went out the front door, I realized I had left my keys in the house. We were completely locked out, and the landlord did not have a spare key. I wasn't sure how we would get back in and thought, *Oh well, I will get to the church, and if anything, I am learning to have joy even during the frustrating times of life.*

The Lord had been speaking to me this very verse in James 1:2-4, "Count it all joy when you fall into various trials, knowing that the testing of your faith produces patience. But let patience have its perfect work, that you may be perfect and complete, lacking nothing" (NKJV).

Thankfully, we got to church, and I was able to share the love of God with many people that day. People received Christ and were healed. Afterwards I thought, *Lord, if I had been a wreck and all stressed out, I might have missed the opportunity to share Your love with these precious people today.*

That's the important thing to realize. When we choose to walk in joy during our journey, we will be sensitive to those around us who need hope and healing. We will be sensitive to those who need to know that Jesus is the only way, truth, and life. But if we are caught up in ourselves and in our problems, we won't be aware of the divine opportunities all around us. We can have joy even during the hard times.

My mom was such a great example of this during the time my dad went on to heaven. She has received strength because her ultimate joy was not based on a person; it was rooted in knowing Jesus. When we know Jesus, we don't sorrow as the world sorrows, because we have hope that we will see our loved ones again some day in heaven. Of course she misses my dad, but she chose not to stay depressed. She chose to get out of bed and continue to live her life for Jesus. She chose to praise God, even in her darkest hour.

The greatest treasure we have is in knowing Jesus and in sharing that incredible gift with those in need. Joy comes when we reach out and love others. "Let your gentleness, be evident to all. The Lord is near" (Philippians 4:5 NIV). People need the love that is inside you. The hope we have in Christ doesn't disappoint because the love of God has been poured into our hearts by the Holy Spirit (Romans 5:5).

You have the love of God inside of you, and the world needs it. So let your gentleness and love be an example to others. Mother Teresa said this: "A joyful heart is the normal result of a heart burning with love. She gives most who gives with joy. Joy is a net of love in which you can catch souls."

Forgiveness

Another key to having joy on the journey is choosing to walk in forgiveness. No matter what people do to us and no matter what they say, Jesus commands us to forgive them. In Mark 11:24-25, He tells us to forgive for our own benefit, so our prayers will not be hindered. You may feel you have the right to be angry with someone for what they have done, but you need to realize it will only hinder your prayers from being answered.

One of the quickest ways we lose our joy is when we begin to let bitterness eat at our hearts. I have heard it said that bitterness is like drinking poison and expecting the other person to die. When we allow jealousy, envy, strife, comparison, dread, fear, hurt, or bitterness to get in our heart, we lose our joy. But when we say, "No, I choose to forgive. I choose to walk in love because of all Jesus has forgiven me of," joy will fill our heart.

There is freedom when we choose to forgive. When we begin to give God thanks for all He has done for us and choose to forgive those who have hurt us, we will walk in a spirit of joy. And that joy gives us strength.

The Umpire of Peace

"Do not be anxious about anything, but in everything, by prayer and petition, with thanksgiving, present your requests to God" (Philippians 4:6 NIV). I don't know everything that's going on in your life or what decisions you are facing concerning your future. But instead of meditating on the concerns you have, cast those cares on the Lord.

Wherever you are, just stop and say, *Lord, I need Your wisdom. I need Your direction. I give You my life and my future. Lord, I ask for Your provision. I ask for Your direction. I ask for Your peace.*

Sometimes it helps me to visualize handing my cares over to God as I pray those things. When we begin to do that and have confidence in our prayers, peace will come in our heart. *"This is the confidence we have in approaching God: that if we ask anything according to his will, he hears us. And if we know that he hears us,...we know that we have what we asked of him"* (1 John 5:14-15 NIV).

The Bible says the prayers of a righteous man are powerful, effective, and avail much. You are righteous because of the blood of Jesus. You can have confidence in His Word and in His promises to meet your needs and to give you the answers you need. So ask Him with confidence. Then take time to wait and ask, *Lord, what are the steps You want me to take?*

I believe God can drop divine wisdom, strategies, and creative ideas in your heart. The Lord gives wisdom to those that ask, so you can ask in faith with confidence and know that He hears you. You can have whatever you ask for according to His will.

The next part of Chapter 4 says "And the peace of God, which transcends all understanding, will guard your hearts and your minds in Christ Jesus" (Philippians 4:7 NIV). People are desperate for peace. We look everywhere in the world to try to find peace of mind. Some go great distances to try to find peace. They might go to another country or to a special vacation destination. Some try to find it in New Eastern meditation. Others try to find peace in a pill, a drug, or a drink. Some even try to find it in another person.

True peace is only found in Jesus. He is the Prince of Peace. That peace is found when we live a life surrendered to Him and cast our cares completely on Him and say, *God, my life is Yours. I trust You that You're working things out together for my good.* "And let the peace (soul harmony which comes) from Christ rule (act as an umpire continually) in your hearts [deciding and settling with finality all the questions that arise in your minds, in that peaceful state] to which as [members of Christ's] one body you were called [to live]. And be thankful (appreciative), [giving praise to God always]" (Colossians 3:15 AMP).

Notice this translation says, "Let the peace of God act as an umpire." The umpire in a baseball game is the one who calls the shots. He tells you whether you are safe or not. In the same way, God's peace should be what calls the shots in our lives. We must let His divine peace direct our lives and give us wisdom on what to do and what not to do. We must choose to refuse doubt, fear, and other things in our lives that would pollute our heart and mind. Then we must choose to walk in the peace, wisdom, and direction of God.

Anytime we get out of peace, which is our divine indicator that pulls us back, we need to get alone with God and say, *What is Your wisdom in this situation? What do I need to do differently? Give me Your direction. I want to be led by Your peace. You call the shots in my life. You are the umpire in my heart. You are the ruler. You are the Lord of my life.*

There are times that we all miss it. I have gotten out of peace and had to say, *Lord, help me. I want to get back into Your peace, divine will, divine plan, and wisdom.* Let the peace of God guard your heart and mind in Christ Jesus. Paul tells us how to keep peace ruling in our hearts. "Finally, brothers, whatever is true, whatever is noble, whatever is right, whatever is pure, whatever is lovely, whatever is admirable – if anything is excellent or praiseworthy – think about such things." (Philippians 4:8 NIV).

Choose to think on what God says about your life, situation, family, finances, etc. Then you will find peace. "Set your mind on things above, not on earthly things" (Colossians 3:2 NIV). Obviously, we all have things we must do on a daily basis that are temporary, but this is saying that we should not fix our attention solely on the natural. We should set our mind on things above. That's where Christ is, and our lives are hidden in Christ.

I remember counseling a girl who said she kept having depressive, suicidal thoughts. She told me, "Well, the thoughts come, so that must mean I should do this. I can't help what comes in my head." I told her, "No that is not true. Those thoughts may come, but you have the ability to change those thoughts and meditate on what God's Word says about you. The more you renew your mind with His thoughts, the more you will realize those thoughts don't come anymore." We have the power to make every thought obedient to what God's Word says (2 Corinthians 10:5). We can take authority over our thought life and imaginations that try to come in our mind.

I was sharing this truth at a women's conference in Hong Kong, and one of the women came up to me afterwards. She was frazzled and said, "I cannot sleep. I'm so tormented. I see demonic spirits all over my room, coming in and out." I began to talk with her more and found that she had previously been involved in ancestor worship, which is very common in that part of the world. So I said, "You need to renounce that old way. You need to make Jesus the Lord of your life. You need to be cleansed by the blood of Jesus, and you can do that right now."

We prayed and she received Jesus as her Lord and Savior. She renounced her old way of life. Then I shared 1 John 4:4 with her, telling her that greater is He that's in you than he that is in this world. I also reminded her that the Spirit of God in her is greater than those demonic spirits that try to torment her, so she needs to command those spirits to leave. She needs to speak the Word. Psalm 4:8 says that perfect peace and rest and sleep can we have because we're His beloved. We can have sweet sleep. We can have rest. It's a promise from God.

The next time I saw her, I didn't even recognize her. She was rested and radiant. She said, "I've been able to sleep ever since then. I haven't seen any evil spirits. I've been taking them captive." Right then, I thought, *This would work in any culture, in any situation.* The Word works!

You can take whatever is holding you back captive and say, *No, I'm not going to dwell on fear. I'm not going to be tormented. I may have a lot on my plate in this new season of my life, but I will not fear.* Begin to speak perfect peace. You can do everything that God has called you to do right now in this season, by the strength and grace of God. He has equipped you, "I can do everything through Him who gives me strength" (Philippians 4:13 NIV). He will enable you to do everything you need to do. When the time comes, He will give you the grace, strength, and courage you need. Trust in Him.

You can have joy on this journey, as you choose to rejoice in every season, walk in gentleness and love toward others, decide not to worry, and pray about everything. Then the peace of God will rule and reign in your heart and mind. When we live according to what the Apostle Paul wrote about by the inspiration of the Holy Spirit, we will walk in joy on our journey. Be encouraged today that God is with you and is leading you. Cast your cares on Him and let Him guide you in every area of your life. Trust His timing because He promises to make all things beautiful in His time. God is faithful.

12

PRESS ON

"Do not throw away your confidence; it will be richly rewarded. You need to persevere so that when you have done the will of God, you will receive what He has promised…we are not those who shrink back and are destroyed, but of those who believe and are saved."

Hebrews 10:35-36,39 NIV

My son Isaac got a new bike for Christmas last year. The one he previously had was a tiny toddler bike, so he had been asking for months for a "big boy" bike. When we took him outside for his first ride on his new bike, we went down a big hill in front of our house. It was exciting for him until we had to turn around and go back up the hill to get home.

It was steep, so he began to get discouraged. When we were halfway up the hill, he dropped his bike and started crying, "I can't do it!" He was ready to leave his bike in the road—*the same bike he had been wanting for several months!* I began to encourage him, "Isaac, don't give up! You can do it! You are stronger than you think, and I'm right beside you to help you!" I got on the other side of the bike and we began pushing it up the hill together. Once we got to the top, he was so happy to see his daddy cheering him on!

Many times in our own lives, we have a dream in front of us--a promise from God--but we want to give up. For some reason or another, it seems too hard to press on. The circumstances and problems look too big for our dream to come to pass. But we must never give up before a breakthrough. "Let us not lose heart and grow weary and faint in acting nobly and doing right, for in due time and at the appointed season we shall reap, if we do not loosen and relax our courage and faint" (Galatians 6:9 AMP).

I like what Jentezen Franklin says in his book, *Take Hold of Your Dream.* He says, "Regret looks back. Worry looks around. Vision looks up! Vision sees the mountain top even when the clouds hide it from view." The story of Joseph in Genesis 37 is a great illustration of the power of a dream. Joseph persevered for years through all kinds of difficulties. For a long time, it seemed as though his dream had died. But God remembered his dream and resurrected it.

We must realize that God's dreams and visions go through a process of birth, death, and resurrection. God uses this process to refine and sanctify us so that, when it comes to pass, He gets the glory. "Count it all joy when you fall into various trials, knowing that the testing of your faith produces patience. But let patience have its perfect work that you may be perfect and complete, lacking nothing" (James 1:2-4 NKJV).

Think about the process a diamond goes through. Before it shines, it is formed by extreme heat and pressure, causing the carbon atoms to crystalize. The pressure built up causes volcanic eruptions that bring the diamonds up after many years. Sometimes the dreams God has put in us go through a similar process of testing. But as we keep our eyes on Jesus and allow Him to work His will in our lives, we will come through shining for His glory!

Don't give up in the process God is taking you through. It may be different than the process someone else is going through, but as you are obedient to Him, you will see the purpose of what He is doing in your life.

Think about the caterpillar. When a caterpillar is in its cocoon, it goes through a process of being transformed into a butterfly. When it is time for it to come out, it has to struggle. If it doesn't struggle to get out, it won't have the strength it needs to fly. In our lives, we may feel like the trials and hardships we face are there to keep us from our destiny. But God can turn those things around for our good if we trust Him.

Another example of this principle can be found in nature—in the Chinese bamboo tree. After the seed is planted, you don't see anything for the first five years. That seed has to be watered consistently, and then at some point during the fifth year, it sprouts and grows up to 90 feet in six weeks! Some may say, *Wow, that grew overnight.* But that's not true. For five years, that seed was growing and strengthening its roots underneath the soil.

Our life is much like the process of a seed being planted. You may not see overnight results, but if you stay faithful, consistent, and patient, the results will soon be manifest. Since we live in a society that is accustomed to instant results, it is difficult for people to be patient.

Continue to seek God first and trust His timing.

There are times we all want to quit or give up, but there is such a great reward for us if we press on. What has God spoken to you? What has He called and assigned you to do? Keep the faith. Don't give up!

Throughout my life, there have been many times I wanted to give up on something that I was in the middle of because I didn't see immediate results. When I was a full-time college student and was also working as a children's pastor and a junior high pastor at my home church, there were many times I wanted to quit. It wasn't always easy. I wasn't sure if I was seeing fruit in the young people's lives we were ministering to. But God reminded me that I was sowing seeds that would produce a harvest.

Many years later, I had young people contact me through letters or phone calls, telling me how grateful they were for me speaking into their lives. I know if I had not been faithful in those things that God had asked me to do, I wouldn't be doing the things I am doing today.

Many times you have to press through the challenges and storms because there are people on the other side. Your dream is not just about you; it's about the people you will influence for the kingdom. It is by faith and patience that we inherit the promises of God! (Hebrews 6:12).

When you stay with God and let Him "grow" you, He will open up new adventures for you to walk in. I remember when we first took our kids to Disney World. Our son, Isaac, wanted to ride the racecar ride so badly, but when we got to the gate, we discovered he was too short to ride. We told him next year he would be tall enough, and we promised to take him back to ride the racecar ride.

Sure enough, the next summer came around, and he reminded us of the promise we had made to him the year before. When we got to Disney World, we went straight to the racecar ride. This time when they measured him, he was tall enough to ride. He was so excited! He had waited and grown to the height required so he could experience the thrill of a new adventure. Likewise, in our lives, as we let God work in us, we will grow in our walk with Him and have new doors of opportunity opened up for us.

Don't Come Down Off the Wall!

In the Bible, there is a story about a man named Nehemiah. Nehemiah heard that the walls of his beloved city, Jerusalem, were broken down and its gates burned. When he heard this, he wept, prayed, and fasted. Then he asked God what to do.

The Jewish people had been exiled from their city, and Nehemiah was living in the citadel of Susa. He went before the king and asked for permission to go back to his home city to rebuild the walls. The king granted him permission, so he went back, gathered the Jewish people and asked them to join him in rebuilding. He assigned every person a position on the wall (Nehemiah 3). There were goldsmiths, merchants, and priests who all took their place working on repairing the wall.

From the very beginning, there were those who criticized and mocked Nehemiah and the people of Jerusalem. Their names were Sanballat, Tobiah, and Geshem. They ridiculed Nehemiah and plotted to stir up trouble against Jerusalem. The people of Jerusalem had to build with a hammer in one hand and wear a sword at their side, as they worked to stay on guard for those trying to attack them.

Their opposition tried to manipulate and distract them from their purpose, but Nehemiah still did not come down off the wall. I'm sure there were times when Nehemiah and his men felt weak, but they pressed on and completed the wall in 52 days (Nehemiah 6:15-16). It was an astounding feat! This is the story in which the famous scripture is found, "The joy of the LORD is your strength" (Nehemiah 8:10). Nehemiah and the people of Israel experienced the revelation of this word for themselves.

As you are pursuing your dream and working in the area God has called you to, there will be those "Sanballats & Tobiahs" who will ridicule and mock you. There will be those who don't understand what God has called you to do, or who just simply don't believe in God. But don't come down off the wall God has called you to build.

My mom wrote a song from this story that has stayed with me. It says, *"Don't come down off the wall you are building for the Lord. Don't come down from praying and standing on God's Word. Though the enemy rage and mock you, trying to make you compromise. Don't come down for you will finish, and your faith will become sized."*

Stay at Your Post

Don't let the enemy distract you from your purpose. We need you to stay on your post. We need every part of the body of Christ to do their part in reaching the harvest.

"Our work as God's servants gets validated—or not—in the details. People are watching us as we stay at our post, alertly, unswervingly . . . in hard times, tough times, bad times; when we're beaten up, jailed, and mobbed; working hard, working late, working without eating; with pure heart, clear head, steady hand; in gentleness, holiness, and honest love; when we're telling the truth, and when God's showing his power; when we're doing our best setting things right; when we're praised, and when we're blamed; slandered, and honored; true to our word, though distrusted; ignored by the world, but recognized by God; terrifically alive, though rumored to be dead; beaten within an inch of our lives, but refusing to die; immersed in tears, yet always filled with deep joy; living on handouts, yet enriching many; having nothing, having it all."

2 Corinthians 6:1-10 MSG

Be faithful where God has put you right now because it is preparation for your future. Be faithful to what God has assigned you to do in this season. I remember my dad sharing with me that when he first started in ministry, he had big dreams and visions of how he wanted to make a difference for Jesus. One day, he came to the Lord in frustration over why things were not happening as quickly as he thought, and the Lord spoke to him and said, "I am more concerned with what I am doing IN YOU than what I can do THROUGH YOU. I am building an oak tree."

God was showing him that just like an acorn starts off small when it is planted, over time as it is rooted and watered, it will grow into a strong oak tree. Trust what God is doing in you. He will prepare you for what He desires to do through you. An oak tree doesn't come up overnight; it has steady growth.

Realize the importance of laying a foundation now, for your future tomorrow. A great example of this is in the building of the CityPlex Towers in Tulsa. One tower is 60 stories tall, another is 30, and the other is 20 stories. These three towers stand next to each other. When they first began to build these buildings, they put beams down, as deep as each building was tall. They took time to make sure the foundation was secure and solid enough to stand the Tulsa weather. In fact, they took much longer to build the foundation than they did the actual building.

Preparation is never lost time. The seeds you plant today will bring a harvest tomorrow. I like the way John Maxwell put it when he said, "Many people overestimate tomorrow and underestimate today. They overestimate the moment of a great accomplishment but underestimate the process that it takes to get you there."

It's easy to compare yourself and the process you are in with others. But realize that God has a specific plan just for you. Don't let anything hold you back from what He has called you to do. Don't let circumstances keep you from fulfilling God's plan for your life. We must be awake to what God is saying. We must put on our strength as we meditate on His Word, shake off the lies of the enemy, and then run the race God has set before us. Don't give up. Hold on to the dream God has given you.

The Ultimate Goal

When I was in 6th grade, I joined the girls' basketball team. I didn't join because I liked to play basketball, but because my dad liked it, and I wanted to please him. I didn't know much about the game or the rules, but I showed up at the first game with my jersey on, thinking I could just *"wing it."*

The 6th grade boys played right before us and Caleb (now my husband) was the star basketball player. He scored most of their points. When it was our turn to play, hundreds of fans were gathered on the bleachers in expectation of a great game. I remember sitting on the bench and halfway through the game, the coach called my name to go in the game. My heart was beating fast, as I quickly ran onto the court. I thought, *If I just run back and forth, it will look like I know what is going on.*

Then suddenly, the ball was thrown to me. The only thing I knew to do was run as fast as I could to the goal and try to score a basket. I was surprised that I had such a clear path, as I was running to the basket. But I kept running and *Swoosh* -- I made a basket! I was so happy! I jumped up and down, screaming. Even I was surprised that I had made the basket.

But as I looked at my teammates, I realized I had made a big mistake. No one else was clapping (except the fans of the opposing team). I had made a basket for the other team! I did not have a clue which goal I was supposed to be aiming for. I was devastated as my classmates laughed at me. Of course, my grandma, who happened to be there, was so kind to pat me on the back and encourage me afterwards,

145

but all I wanted to do was duck my head and leave as quickly as possible. Thankfully, Caleb didn't marry me for my basketball skills!

The point of this story is that so many times we can be going back and forth in the "game of life," aiming at the wrong goal. We may be aiming at the goal of pleasing people, having a certain image, or just focusing on things that are temporary. If we are aiming at one of these goals, then when we come to the end of our lives, we will realize that's not what life is about.

When we first moved to Hong Kong, God brought this experience to my mind. I was walking down the street to the grocery market, worried about decisions we needed to make. Then God asked me, *"Sarah, who are you seeking to please? What is your goal? Is your goal to please others? Or is your goal to be obedient to me and reach people with my love?"*

> *So we make it our goal to please him… For Christ's love compels us because we are convinced that one died for all,…and those who live should no longer live for themselves but for him who died for them and was raised again.*
>
> 2 Corinthians 5:9,14-15 NIV

When we live with an eternal perspective, we no longer fear what people think. We live to please God and to make Him known in the earth. "We fix our eyes not on what is seen, but on what is unseen. For what is seen is temporary, but what is unseen is eternal" (2 Corinthians 4:18 NIV).

Now is the time to wake up and rise up to your divine assignment. You have a job to do for the kingdom of God. So don't let fear, bitterness, or tragedy from your past keep you from the purpose God has for you. Take up God's strength, shake off the lies of the enemy, and begin using what God has put in your hand.

As you offer God what's in your hand, He will do extraordinary things through your life. Remember to travel light, trust His timing, and enjoy the journey. God is faithful to complete what He has started in you, so never give up. This is your time to rise up to your divine assignment!

Endnotes

Chapter 2

[1] Page. 28. A Deeper Level, Whitaker House (Publisher), New Kensington, PA 2007, Page. 118.

[2] Page. 40. "Distant Relatives" story by Carl Muir.

Chapter 6

[1] Page. 68. Story by Peter Marshall

[2] Page. 69. (W.E. Vine, Vine's Complete Expository Dictionary of Old and New Testament Words. Nashville: Thomas Nelson Publishers, 1996. Page 524).

SALVATION PRAYER

As you have read this book, my prayer is that you have gained a greater revelation of God's love for you. No matter who you are, no matter what your past, God loves you so much that He gave His one and only begotten Son for you. The Bible tells us that "...everyone who believes in him will not perish but have eternal life" (John 3:16 NLT). Jesus laid down His life and rose again so that we could spend eternity with Him in heaven and expereince His absolute best on earth. If you would like to receive Jesus into your life, pray this prayer out loud and mean it from your heart.

Heavenly Father, I come to You admitting that I am a sinner. Right now, I choose to turn away from sin, and I ask You to cleanse me of all unrighteousness. I believe that Your Son, Jesus, died on the cross to take away my sins. I also believe that He rose again from the dead so that I might be forgiven of my sins and be made righteous through faith in Him. I call upon the name of Jesus Christ to be the Savior and Lord of my life. Jesus, I choose to follow You and ask that You fill me with the power of the Holy Spirit. I declare that right now I am a child of God. I am free from sin and full of the righteousness of God. I am saved in Jesus' name. Amen.

ABOUT THE AUTHOR

Sarah Wehrli is a passionate speaker with a heart to encourage people in their God-given purpose. She has served in leadership at her home church for 13 years and ministered in 30 nations. She is the co-founder with her husband, Caleb, of Inspire International, a ministry focused on evangelizing the lost and equipping leaders globally. They started Hope for Children initiatives, which focus on providing housing and relief to orphans and children at risk in Asia. Sarah and her husband, Caleb, have two children.

FOR THE CHILDREN

When God spoke to my heart to write this book in January of 2012, I knew the purpose of this book was not only to awaken the body of Christ to their assignment, but also for the children God has called us to rescue in other nations. He spoke to my heart, "Write for the children." As I have shared in the book, we established a mission organization, Hope for Children, to build orphanages, support rescue homes for trafficked victims, build water wells, and provide feeding programs for children in Asia. The proceeds received from this book will go towards our Hope for Children initiatives around the world.

James 1:27 New Living Translation, *"Pure and genuine religion in the sight of God the Father means caring for orphans and widows in their distress and refusing to let the world corrupt you."*

Isaiah 52:7 Amplified Bible, *"How beautiful upon the mountains are the feet of him who brings good tidings, who **publishes** peace, who brings good tidings of good, who **publishes** salvation, who says to Zion, Your God reigns!"*

Mark 16:15 Amplified Bible, "And He said to them, Go into all the world and preach and ***publish openly the good news (the Gospel) to every creature [of the whole human race]."***

Thank you for making a difference in the children of the world!

HOPE
FOR CHILDREN

Hope for Children exists to help meet the spiritual and physical needs of hurting children in various places around the world.

INSPIRE**INTERNATIONAL**INITIATIVES

- Orphanages

- Water Wells

- Food Distribution

- Supporting rescue homes for victims of human trafficking

www.inspireintl.com

EVANGELIZE
ENCOURAGE
EQUIP

www.inspireintl.com